Also by Doreen Rappaport

LIVING DANGEROUSLY
American Women Who Risked Their Lives for Adventure

ESCAPE FROM SLAVERY
Five Journeys to Freedom

AMERICAN WOMEN
Their Lives in Their Words

THE BOSTON COFFEE PARTY

TROUBLE AT THE MINES

Be the Judge **?** Be the Jury
THE SACCO-VANZETTI TRIAL

BE THE JUDGE? BE THE JURY™
THE LIZZIE BORDEN TRIAL
DOREEN RAPPAPORT

ILLUSTRATED WITH
PHOTOGRAPHS, PRINTS
AND DIAGRAMS

HarperCollinsPublishers

Grateful acknowledgment is made to the following for the use of photographs
in this book:
The Bettmann Archive: 158. Culver Pictures, Inc.: 16, 126, 150. Fall River
Historical Society: 8, 13, 14, 40, 48, 58, 59, 60, 72, 99, 139, 141. Edwin H.
Porter, *The Fall River Tragedy*: 27, 28, 96, 132, 142. *New York Daily Tribune*: 70,
June 13, 1893. New York Public Library: 122, 88. *The New York Recorder*: 25,
June 5, 1893; 33, June 7, 1893; 63, June 5, 1893; 64, June 10, 1893; 83, June
15, 1893; 93, June 5, 1893; 103, June 7, 1893. *The Sun*: 160, June 21, 1893.

The Lizzie Borden Trial

Library of Congress Cataloging-in-Publication Data
Rappaport, Doreen.
    The Lizzie Borden trial / Doreen Rappaport ; illustrated with photo-
graphs, prints, and diagrams.
        p.   cm. — (Be the judge / be the jury)
    Summary: A reconstruction of the Lizzie Borden trial, using testimony
from edited transcripts of the trial, during which the reader can assume the
role of juror.
    ISBN 0-06-025113-1. — ISBN 0-06-025114-X (lib. bdg.)
    1. Borden, Lizzie, 1860–1927—Trials, litigation, etc.—Juvenile literature.
2. Trials (Murder)—Massachusetts—New Bedford—Juvenile literature.
[1. Borden, Lizzie, 1860–1927—Trials, litigation, etc.   2. Trials (Murder)]
I. Title.   II. Series: Rappaport, Doreen.   Be the judge/be the jury.
KF223.B6R36   1992   91-23232
345.73' 02523' 0974485—dc20   CIP
[347.30525230974485]   AC

1   2   3   4   5   6   7   8   9   10 ❖
First Edition

Diagrams by Meera Kothari
Logo icons by Chris Cart

For Bob Rosenblum—
master spinner of suspense, mentor and cherished friend

Contents

Everything in this book really happened. This book contains the actual testimony of the witnesses at the Lizzie Borden trial.

Andrew Borden, murdered August 4, 1892

Before the Trial

The Crime

On August 4, 1892, in Fall River, Massachusetts, Andrew Borden and his wife, Abby, were murdered. Both deaths were caused by wounds from a sharp, heavy weapon such as a hatchet or an ax. Mr. Borden received ten wounds on his head; Mrs. Borden, nineteen wounds on her head and one on the back of her neck. Eight days later, Lizzie Borden, Mr. Borden's thirty-two-year-old daughter from his first marriage, was accused of both murders. Ten months later, her trial began.

It became headline news in the United States and in Europe. People were shocked by the possibility that a wealthy woman from a respected family might have committed these brutal murders.

For as long as it takes you to read this book, you will BE THE JURY at Lizzie Borden's trial. You will sit in the jury box and listen to witnesses testify and be cross-examined. You will evaluate the evidence and decide whether or not Lizzie Borden murdered her father and stepmother.

Read carefully. Think carefully about everything you read. Do not make your decision lightly, for you hold Lizzie Borden's life in your hands.

Who Were the Bordens?

Lizzie's father, Andrew Borden, was a rich businessman. His great-grandfather and other members of the family had once owned most of Fall River, a town fifty miles from Boston and twenty miles from Providence, Rhode Island. But Andrew's father had lost much of the family's money. Andrew vowed to earn back his family's fortune. Through smart and often ruthless business deals, he became one of the richest men in Fall River.

In 1845 Andrew married a farm girl, Sarah J. Morse. Four years later, their first daughter,

Emma, was born. A second daughter, Alice, died a year after her birth. A third daughter, Lizzie Andrew, was born in 1860. (Andrew had wanted a son and insisted that Lizzie's middle name be what the boy's name would have been.) In 1863 Sarah Morse Borden died.

Two years later, Andrew married Abby Durfee Gray, although he did not love her the

Andrew   Abby

way he loved his first wife. It was a marriage of convenience. Abby became his wife and step-mother to sixteen-year-old Emma and five-year-old Lizzie.

At the time of the murder, Lizzie lived with her family. Her daily life was like that of most rich single women at the turn of the century. She visited with her friends, did charity work at church, taught a Sunday-school class, and was active in the Women's Christian Temperance Union. She took a trip to Europe with a friend in 1890.

How Did Lizzie Borden Get to Trial?

Investigation: August 4, 1892

The police searched the Borden house and grounds for possible weapons and objects relating to the crime. They photographed the victims in their surroundings. They questioned family members, neighbors, and other people near the scene of the crime. The medical examiner performed autopsies. The police did not inspect the person or clothing of Lizzie on the day of the murders. Fingerprinting was not used in Fall River then.

Inquest: August 8–11, 1892

The inquest was closed to the public. Lizzie and others who had been questioned before were questioned again. Police officers testified about what they had seen and learned. The prosecutor studied the testimony and concluded that Lizzie had murdered her father and stepmother.

The Arrest: August 11, 1892

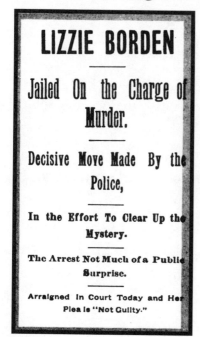

LIZZIE BORDEN

Jailed On the Charge of Murder.

Decisive Move Made By the Police,

In the Effort To Clear Up the Mystery.

The Arrest Not Much of a Public Surprise.

Arraigned In Court Today and Her Plea Is "Not Guilty."

Lizzie was arrested and put in jail. In Massachusetts in 1892, a person accused of murder could not be released on bail. Bail is money deposited by accused persons to guarantee they will return for the trial.

Headlines from *Fall River Daily Globe*

Preliminary Hearing: August 22, 1892

Again the police and other witnesses testified. The prosecutor hoped their evidence would convince the judge that there was *probable cause*, or reasonable grounds, for believing that Lizzie was the murderer. Lizzie and her lawyer attended the hearing and heard the evidence against her. The judge decided that there was probable cause to believe that she was guilty. She was taken back to her cell until the grand jury met.

Grand Jury: December 8, 1892

The grand jury of twenty-one men was selected from voter registration rolls. (In 1892 women did not yet have the right to vote.) Because defendants and their lawyers are not allowed to attend grand jury proceedings, the grand jury heard only prosecution witnesses and then the prosecution's summary of the case. The grand jury decided that there was enough evidence to bring Lizzie to trial. It issued an indictment charging her with first-degree murder.

First-degree murder is generally a killing that has been *premeditated* (thought out beforehand). The penalty for first-degree murder was death.

The Arraignment: May 8, 1893

Lizzie entered a formal plea of *not guilty* to the charges of murder. Her trial was set for June 6, 1893.

What Are the Rights of an Accused Murderer Under the Constitution?

Fourth Amendment. Without permission or a search warrant, Lizzie's home cannot be searched and articles in it cannot be taken. A search warrant was not necessary because Lizzie consented to the search.

Fifth Amendment. Lizzie must be charged by a grand jury. If the grand jury decides there is enough evidence to bring her to trial, it issues an indictment.

Lizzie cannot be forced to testify against herself. She cannot be convicted without *due process*: fair legal procedures must be followed.

Sixth Amendment. Lizzie must have a speedy and public trial. She must be informed of all charges against her. She must cross-examine witnesses against her and have time to present witnesses in her favor. She has the right to have a lawyer represent her.

Eighth Amendment. There may be no excessively high bail or fines or "cruel and unusual punishment."

What Is a Trial?

The trial is like a contest between two opponents: the prosecutor represents the state and the defense lawyer represents the defendant. In a criminal trial, the state brings charges against the accused (defendant). The prosecutor tries to convince the jury that the defendant is guilty of the charges beyond a reasonable doubt. The defense lawyer tries to dispute the charges and show that there is reasonable doubt that the defendant is guilty.

The official name for the trial is the *Commonwealth of Massachusetts versus Lizzie Borden*. In the United States, a person is considered innocent until proven guilty by a trial—even though a judge has found probable cause and a grand jury has made an indictment.

What Does the Prosecutor Do?

In 1893 in Massachusetts, the prosecutor prepared search warrants and arrest warrants. After questioning witnesses at the inquest, he decided that there was enough evidence to bring Lizzie to trial.

The prosecutor spoke at the preliminary hearing and convinced the judge of probable cause. He convinced the grand jury to indict Lizzie. His job at the trial is to prove that she is guilty beyond a reasonable doubt.

What Does the Defense Lawyer Do?

As soon as Lizzie knew she was suspected, she hired Andrew Jennings, her family's lawyer. He told her what to say and what not to say during the inquest, the arraignment, and the preliminary hearing.

Jennings hired two other lawyers to help him. They looked for witnesses to establish reasonable doubt of Lizzie's guilt and to contradict evidence of prosecution witnesses. At the trial, the defense lawyers cross-examined the prosecution's witnesses and tried to punch holes in their evidence; later they presented their case with their own witnesses.

What Does the Judge Do?

Judges should not take sides. They listen to evidence and make sure that a defendant's constitutional rights are protected and that proper procedures are followed. When the lawyers argue over evidence, the judge listens and, based on rules about evidence, decides whether or not the evidence should be admitted. In 1893 in Massachusetts, three judges were required at criminal cases in Superior Court.

What Does the Jury Do?

A jury listens to the evidence to decide whether it proves beyond a reasonable doubt that the defendant is guilty. Jury members may not talk about the case with anyone. They are not allowed to read newspaper accounts about the trial. They try to stay impartial (unprejudiced) about the case. Lizzie's jury was sequestered; they were not allowed to go home during the trial.

What Does the Defendant Do?

Lizzie has the right to be in court every day of the trial, but she does not have to testify. The Massachusetts Constitution and the Fifth Amendment to the U.S. Constitution state that in criminal cases defendants do not have to testify. The fact that Lizzie might not choose to testify may not be interpreted to mean that she is guilty.

Lizzie's presence in court is important. What she wears, how she looks, how she carries herself and responds to what goes on during the trial affect what the jury thinks of her and may affect its verdict.

Who Took Part in Lizzie's Trial?

Chief Justice Albert Mason
Associate Justice Caleb Blodgett
Associate Justice Justin Dewey

Clerk

Witness Stand

12 Jurors

THE DEFENSE
Andrew Jennings
Melvin O. Adams
George D. Robinson

THE PROSECUTION
Hosea M. Knowlton
William H. Moody

Choosing the Jury

Monday, June 5, 1893

By the time Lizzie's trial started, she had been in jail ten months. Newspapers all over the world had headlined the crime. Over thirty reporters came to New Bedford, Massachusetts, to cover the trial. Western Union had to install ten new wires in town so reporters could get their stories in each day.

The sidewalk outside the courthouse was choked with curious citizens, mostly women, eager for even a glimpse of Lizzie. At 9 A.M. the reporters joined the lucky spectators who were also allowed into the courtroom. At 11 A.M. Lizzie arrived, with the sheriff. They had trouble wending their way through the large crowd still outside the courthouse.

Lizzie stood five feet, four inches and

WHO KILLED THE BORDENS ?

Miss Lizzie Borden Put on Trial at New Bedford To-
Day for the Slaughter of Her Father and Stepmother—The Most Mysterious Crime
of American Criminal History.

A CASE THAT THE WHOLE WORLD WILL WATCH

Headlines from *The New York Recorder*

weighed 135 pounds. Her reddish hair was
parted in the middle and combed back behind
her ears. Despite the day's insufferable heat,
she wore a high-collared black brocade dress.
The sleeves puffed at the shoulders and tapered
down to her wrists. A large white feather was
among the five black ones jutting up from her
black hat. In her gloved hands was a closed
black fan.

Lizzie sat down next to her lawyers. The
Reverends Jubb and Buck of the Central Con-
gregational Church of Fall River came over to
greet her. A few of Lizzie's women friends came
over to say hello, too. Lizzie's sister, Emma,
was not in the courtroom; as a defense witness

she was not permitted to be there before testifying so as not to be influenced by the other witnesses' statements. The three judges entered, and everyone in the courtroom rose.

Jury selection began. Names had been picked at random from the registered voters of the county. It is hoped that jurors know little or nothing about a case, so they can be fair. But the Borden murders had been so widely publicized that the lawyers knew that almost all the jurors would have read something about it.

To eliminate jurors who were prejudiced, Chief Justice Mason questioned each man. Among the questions he asked was: "Have you formed any opinions that would prevent you from reaching a fair verdict?"

A number of times the lawyers challenged a juror. When Justice Mason agreed that the juror had revealed something showing that he could not come to a fair verdict, he excused the juror. At other times, the lawyers asked that a juror be excused without telling the reason. Each side has the right to a certain number of challenges, which are used when no concrete objection can be made but the lawyer feels uncomfortable about a juror.

By the end of the day, 12 men had been chosen from among the 108 questioned and were sworn in as jurors.

The Prosecution's Opening Statement

Tuesday, June 6, 1893

An opening statement reviews the crime and summarizes what the prosecutor intends to prove. Prosecutors hope their openings are effective, because they want to impress the jury with their side of the case even at this early moment in the trial.

Forty-year-old William H. Moody had been the district attorney for Essex County for two years. He was known as a hardworking, careful lawyer. He rose from his chair and buttoned his coat. He glanced down at a large pile of typewritten notes on the table in front of him, then walked toward the jury. Lizzie's face reddened as he began to speak.

On August fourth of last year, an old man and woman, husband and wife, each without a known enemy in the world, were killed in their own home, on a busy street, during daylight. First one, then the other. The daughter of one of the victims is accused of these crimes.

Five years ago bad feelings developed between the prisoner and her stepmother. Up to that time Lizzie had addressed her as "Mother." From that time on she stopped. I know of nothing more significant of the bad feeling between them than the prisoner's comments to a police officer shortly after the homicides were discovered. While her parents lay at the very place they had fallen under the blows of the assassin, a police officer asked Miss Borden, "When did you last see your mother?" And the prisoner replied, "She is not my mother. She is my stepmother. My mother is dead." You will learn that though this family lived in the same house, there were locks and bolts and bars between their rooms.

Tuesday night, two days before the murder, Mr. and Mrs. Borden were ill with violent vomiting. Supposedly the prisoner was affected, too. The servant was not. On Wednesday the prisoner went to buy prussic acid, a dangerous poison. That same evening, she told her friend Alice Russell she was worried that something terrible was going to happen to her family.

On the morning of the murders Mr. Borden and John Morse, the prisoner's uncle, left the house by nine o'clock. Shortly after the servant Bridget went outside to wash the windows. Mrs. Borden went upstairs to make the bed in the guest room. After a bit Lizzie went upstairs, too. From the time Mrs. Borden went upstairs and was murdered, to the time the prisoner came downstairs an hour later, there was no one else in the house but the prisoner, no one else who had the opportunity to kill her.

Mr. Borden came home about 10:15 A.M. He was surprised to find the front door locked and bolted. It was usually only closed by a spring lock. Bridget opened the door for him. The prisoner, who was upstairs, heard her father come in and laughed. Then she walked past the guest room where her stepmother lay dead on the floor and went down the stairs to greet him. To cut off any questions about Mrs. Borden, she lied to her father. She said Mrs. Borden had left the house on an errand. Mr. Borden went to lie down in the sitting room. Lizzie tried to get Bridget to leave the house by telling her about a sale of cotton goods. But Bridget didn't go. She finished washing the windows and then went upstairs to her room. Soon after, the prisoner called up to Bridget that her father was dead. After the murder the prisoner went upstairs to her room and changed her dress.

Before anyone suspected the prisoner, everyone asked her the same question: "Where were you when your father was murdered?" As more people asked where she had been, her story changed. She said she was in the barn but her alibi does not hold. The day of the murder was one of the hottest days in history. By 11 A.M. in the morning it was one hundred degrees. The heat in the barn was unbearable. Officer Medley examined the barn-loft floor. It was thickly covered with dust. There were no footprints there, because the prisoner had not been there.

The police found a hatchet whose handle had been broken off. The break was fresh. The blade was covered with coarse dust. The blade of the weapon that killed Mr. Borden was three and a half inches, exactly the size of this handleless hatchet.

Much blood was spattered about the rooms where the murders took place. Some blood had to get on the assailant or on his or her clothing. Here is the dark-blue silk dress the prisoner said she wore the morning of the murders. An expert found no blood on it. After Dr. Bowen and Mrs. Churchill testify, you will be convinced that Miss Borden did not wear this silk dress that morning. Instead she wore a light-blue cotton dress with a navy-blue diamond figure on it.

On Saturday night, Lizzie Borden learned that she was under suspicion. On Sunday morning, she burned a light-blue dress with a navy-blue figure on it. She had worn that dress most mornings.

When the bodies were found, nothing in the house had been disturbed. No property had been taken. No drawers had been ransacked. Mr. Borden had a large sum of money on him. He was a wealthy man. The assailant approached each victim in broad daylight and without a struggle or a murmur laid them low. No one was seen entering or escaping from any side of the house. The murderer was someone who knew the house and its occupants well.

In the days that follow, listen to the evidence and decide whether there is any other reasonable explanation for these murders other than the prisoner's guilt.

Moody paused, then turned and bowed to the judges. "I call Thomas Kiernan to the stand."

Lizzie fell back in her chair. Spectators wondered whether she had fainted. Her lawyer Andrew Jennings put smelling salts under her nose, then gave her some water to drink. She looked better. The judge called a short recess.

FELL IN A FAINT

———

MOODY'S AWFUL ARRAIGNMENT

———

The Prosecution Promises to Offer Some Strong Evidence Against Miss Borden—The Jurors Visit the Scene of the Tragedy at Fall River.

Headlines from *The New York Recorder*

What Evidence Is Allowed at a Trial?

Each side presents *witnesses* whose testimony tends to support its side of the case. All testimony must clearly relate to the main issue. Generally, witnesses cannot give their opinions.

Some witnesses give *direct* evidence; they testify to what they have seen ("I saw her shoot the victim"). Sometimes witnesses give *circumstantial* evidence; they testify to the circumstances around the crime, and the jury draws conclusions from these circumstances. In Lizzie's case, her behavior before and after the murders was circumstantial evidence.

Expert witnesses are sometimes police officers, medical examiners, and toxicologists (specialists in poisons). Experts may interpret evidence and give their opinions.

Be the Jury

Now listen to the evidence and search for the truth. Remember that even though Lizzie has been arrested and charged with murder, she is still presumed to be innocent. The government does *not* have to prove Lizzie guilty beyond all *possibility* of a doubt, but rather the prosecution must establish her guilt beyond a *reasonable* doubt. The defense doesn't have to prove that she is innocent. The defense only needs to point out flaws in incriminating evidence to convince the jury that her guilt was not proved.

What is a reasonable doubt? A doubt for which some reason can be given. The doubt must come from the evidence or from the lack of evidence. It cannot come from the fact that there are other solutions to the crime that are just as believable. A doubt cannot be based on a guess or whim or thought unrelated to the evidence. A doubt cannot be based on sympathy for Lizzie or a belief that her act should not be illegal, or from the jury's wish to avoid the disagreeable job of convicting her.

The Prosecution's Strategy

In trying to prove Lizzie guilty beyond a reasonable doubt the prosecution will present evidence to establish:

- Lizzie's *motive* for the murders;
- her *premeditation* (design or plan to kill);
- her *opportunity* to commit the crime;
- that she had the *means* (weapon) and *capacity* (physical strength) to commit the crime;
- that her *actions* after the crime (lying, concealing information, destroying suspicious material) showed her guilt;
- that her *alibi* did not hold.

The Defense's Strategy

In trying to prove Lizzie not guilty beyond a reasonable doubt, the defense will cross-examine the prosecution's witnesses, hoping to cast doubt on their testimony. The defense will challenge whether the witness's story is accurate or believable. Sometimes the defense will try to show that the witness told a different story about the same thing at another time. The defense will also suggest other explanations for damaging testimony. These explanations will be more fully developed when the defense presents its case.

Prosecution Witnesses

Witness: Thomas Kiernan
Direct Examination by the Prosecution

Kiernan, an engineer, showed and explained his drawings of the inside and outside of the Borden house. He also noted the distances between the house and places on Main Street that Mr. Borden visited on the day of the murders. These trial exhibits would be used when needed during the trial.

Cross-Examination by the Defense

Kiernan's evidence showed that Lizzie wouldn't necessarily have noticed Mrs. Borden's body when she walked up or down the stairs or past the room.

Q. Did you conduct any experiments at the house?
A. Yes. I had my assistant lie down on the floor in the guest bedroom, right where Mrs. Borden's body

was found. He's much taller than she was. His feet projected past the bed while Mrs. Borden's hadn't. Then I walked up the stairs. I stopped on each step and looked into the guest room. I didn't see my assistant on the floor, even though I knew he was there. On one step, I saw him. But I really think I saw him because I knew he was there and I deliberately looked for him.

Q. When you were in the hall upstairs, in front of Miss Lizzie's room, did you see your assistant?

A. No, I couldn't see any portion of his body.

The defense suggested the possibility of an unknown assailant:

Q. Was the closet in the front hall large enough to hide a person?

A. Yes, sir.

Be the Jury

If Kiernan, who was looking for a body, hadn't seen it when going up or down the stairs, why should Lizzie have seen Mrs. Borden's body?

Next, the jury, along with the judges, the prosecutors, and the defense lawyers, went to inspect the Borden house. Jurors sometimes visit the scene of a crime, because this firsthand look helps them better understand what took place as they hear the evidence.

The Borden house was a white clapboard house on Second Street, a busy street outside the city's main business area. Most wealthy families in Fall River did not live in this part of town. They lived up on "The Hill," in large homes with fine views of the city.

The Borden house was very narrow, with a narrow yard around it. In the front was a picket fence with two gates. The small barn in the back of the house was surrounded by a high fence with barbed wire on the top and bottom. The house had three doors. The front door led into a hall. The side door led into a hall that led into the kitchen. The third door led down to the cellar.

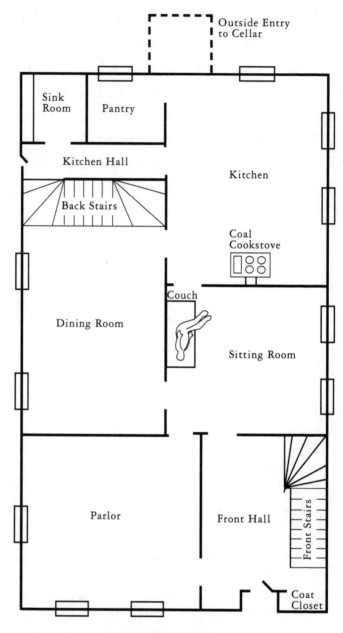

Outside Entry
to Cellar

Sink
Room

Pantry

Kitchen Hall

Kitchen

Back Stairs

Coal
Cookstove

Couch

Dining Room

Sitting Room

Parlor

Front Hall

Front Stairs

Coat
Closet

First Floor

The jury was taken through the house. It was lit by kerosene lamps. There was a cold-water faucet just inside the kitchen door and one in the cellar. The only toilet in the house was in the cellar.

Mr. Borden was killed on the couch in the sitting room on the ground floor.

Be the Jury

If the Bordens were so rich, why didn't they have electric lights, like other wealthy people in Fall River?

If the Bordens were so rich, why didn't they have bathrooms on every floor?

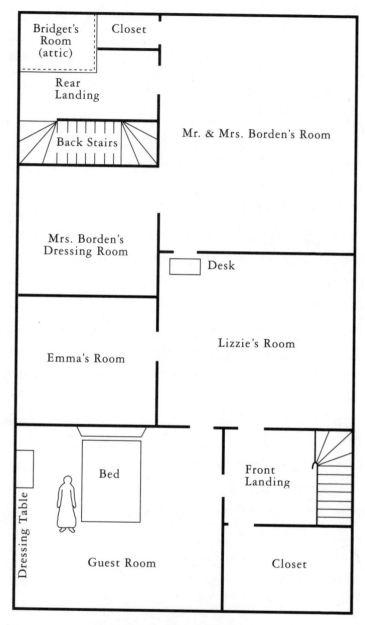

Second Floor

At the top of the stairs on the second floor, it was possible to look into the guest room if the door was open. Mrs. Borden was killed in this guest room. All bedrooms were kept locked with keys. There was little privacy or space between the bedrooms. The front stairs led to a closet, the guest bedroom, and Lizzie's bedroom. Lizzie's sister Emma had to go through Lizzie's bedroom to get to her bedroom.

Lizzie's parents could get to their bedroom only by the back stairs. The door between their room and Lizzie's was always locked on both sides. Lizzie also had a desk pushed against the door to her parents' bedroom.

Bridget got to her attic bedroom by a steep narrow staircase in the rear of the house.

Be the Jury

Why were all the bedroom doors locked?

Why didn't Fall River's most wealthy citizen live better?

Could Mr. Borden's stinginess be a possible motive for Lizzie to murder him?

Wednesday, June 7, 1893
Witness: John V. Morse
Direct Examination by the Prosecution

Morse, Lizzie's uncle, was the brother of Mr. Borden's first wife. He was visiting at the time of the murders. The prosecutor wanted to show that Lizzie avoided spending time at home.

Q. Who did you see on August third?

A. I arrived about 1:30 P.M. and saw Mr. and Mrs. Borden and Bridget. About 3 P.M. I went to Swansea. I returned about 8:30 P.M. I never saw Lizzie at all that day or night.

Q. Did you see her on the day of the murders?

A. No. Her door was closed when I went down in the morning. I didn't see her from the time I arrived on Wednesday until I returned to the house on Thursday, after the murders.

Q. When you visited four weeks ago, did you see her?

A. No, not at all.

Cross-Examination by the Defense

The defense wanted to minimize Lizzie's absences at home and to cast doubt on whether the front door was deliberately locked from the inside.

Q. Did you see Bridget at dinner?

A. No, sir.

Q. You left the house about 3 P.M. and returned about 8:40 P.M. Did you see Bridget when you returned?

A. No, sir.

Q. What have you noticed about the spring lock on the front door?

A. If you shut the door hard, the spring lock catches. If you don't, it doesn't catch and you can open it without any trouble.

Be the Jury

Was Lizzie out so much because she didn't like being at home?

Was the door deliberately or accidentally locked from the inside?

Witness: **Bridget Sullivan**

Twenty-six-year-old Sullivan had worked as a housekeeper for the Bordens for two years and nine months. She entered the courtroom wearing a stylish maroon dress and a big matching hat with a plume feather and leather gloves. The outfit was that of a lady, not a servant. Lizzie stiffened in her seat when Bridget was called to the witness stand.

Direct Examination by the Prosecution

Sullivan revealed that Lizzie had had the sole opportunity to kill Mrs. Borden, since she had been the only person in the house when Mrs. Borden was murdered.

Q. Please tell us what happened the morning of the murders.

A. I came down at 6:15 A.M. and started the fire. I unlocked the back door, took in the milk, hooked the screen door, and started breakfast. About 6:30 Mrs. Borden came downstairs. Mr. Borden appeared about five minutes later. Mr. Morse came shortly after. I served breakfast and cleaned up. Mr. Borden let Mr. Morse out by the back door. He hooked the screen door after him.

Five minutes later Miss Lizzie came down. I was feeling nauseous so I went outdoors. I came back about fifteen minutes later and hooked the screen door. About 9 A.M. Mrs. Borden called me into the sitting room and told me to wash the windows inside and outside. I didn't see her after that until I found her dead upstairs.

I cleaned up more in the kitchen, went to the cellar for a pail of water, then went outside. Miss Lizzie called to me from the back door. She said she would be outside, so I didn't have to bother locking the door. But if I wanted to lock it I could.

I went outside and talked at the fence for a bit with Mrs. Kelly's girl. Then I washed all the outside windows. While I was outside I didn't see anybody go into the house. When I was washing the sitting-room windows, I didn't see anyone through them. I came inside and hooked the screen door.

Sullivan's testimony led to the puzzling question of why the front door, which was usually not bolted from the inside during the day, was bolted that day; the prosecution believed this was part of Lizzie's murder plan.

I heard a noise at the front door, like someone was trying to unlock it but couldn't. I went to the front door and unbolted it. I unlocked all three locks, including the spring lock, which usually wasn't locked. While I was doing it, I said, "Oh pshaw." I heard Miss Lizzie laughing upstairs. I let Mr. Borden in.

Lizzie told Sullivan that a note had come for Mrs. Borden. This note was never found by the police in all their searches. Newspaper articles had asked for the writer of the note to come forward. Emma and Lizzie had also advertised and asked the person to step forward. No one responded. The prosecutor thought Lizzie had lied about the note and that her lie showed her guilt.

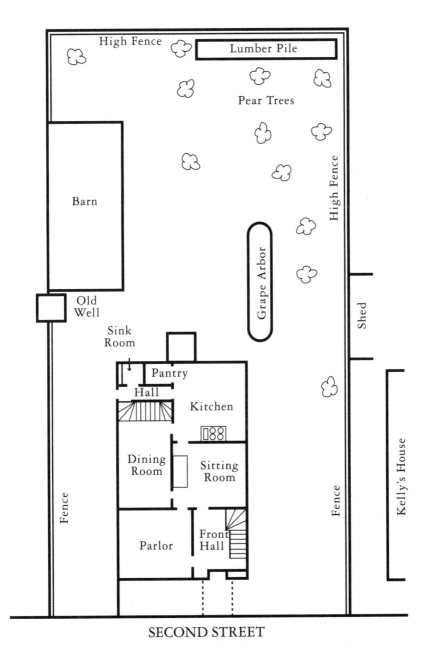

The Borden House and Yard

Q. When did you next see Lizzie?

A. She came downstairs. She told her father that Mrs. Borden had received a note and had gone out. He took his bedroom key off the mantelpiece and went up the back stairs. When he came down, Miss Lizzie and I were in the dining room. She was ironing handkerchiefs. She asked me if I was planning to go out in the afternoon.

I said I didn't know. She said, "If you go out, lock the door, because Mrs. Borden has gone out on a sick call, and I might go out, too." I said, "Who's sick?" She said, "I don't know. She had a note this morning from someone in town." I hadn't seen anyone come with a note.

I finished my work and went into the kitchen. Mr. Borden went into the sitting room to lie down. Miss Lizzie came in and told me about a sale of dress goods at Sargeant's. I told her I wanted to go, but I wasn't feeling so well, so I went upstairs to my room.

The prosecutor believed that Lizzie mentioned the sale to get Bridget out of the house so she could murder her father.

Q. What happened after you went upstairs?

A. I lay down on my bed. I heard the City Hall bell ring eleven times. About eleven minutes or so later, I heard Miss Lizzie holler, "Bridget, come down; come down quick! Father's dead—somebody came in and killed him!" I ran downstairs. Miss Lizzie was standing with her back to the screen door. I started to go into the sitting room but she stopped me. "I need a doctor quick," she said. "Go over to Dr. Bowen's house. Now!" He wasn't home but I left a message with his wife.

When I came back, Miss Lizzie said, "Go get Miss Russell. I can't be alone in the house." I asked her where she had been when the murder occurred. She said she had been in the yard, heard a groan, and rushed in. I went to get Miss Russell. She wasn't in. When I returned, a neighbor, Mrs. Churchill, was there. I suggested going to Mrs. Borden's sister. I thought she might know where Mrs. Borden was. Then Miss Lizzie said, "I am almost positive I heard her come in. Will you go upstairs to see?" I said.

Mrs. Churchill went up with me. When we reached the top of the stairs, I saw Mrs. Borden lying facedown on the guest-room floor. I ran into the room and stood at the foot of the bed. Mrs. Churchill didn't go into the room. We both came right downstairs.

Be the Jury

Who else but Lizzie had the opportunity to kill Mrs. Borden?

Who else but Lizzie or Bridget had the opportunity to kill Mr. Borden?

Why was the front door bolted from the inside?

Why didn't Lizzie scream or show more emotion after she discovered her father?

Cross-Examination by the Defense

The defense did not want the jury to think that there was trouble in the family because they might think this trouble was Lizzie's motive for Mrs. Borden's murder.

Q. Was the Borden house a pleasant place to live?
A. Yes, sir, I liked the place.
Q. Did you ever see any conflict or quarreling in the family?
A. No, sir, I didn't see any. One time though, when Mrs. Borden was sick, neither daughter went to her room to see her.
Q. Did the daughters eat with their parents?
A. Sometimes, but most of the time they didn't. They got up later than their parents. So more often they didn't eat breakfast together. Sometimes they

ate dinner together. A good many more times not.

Q. Did you ever hear Miss Lizzie talking with her mother?

A. Yes, sir. She always spoke to Mrs. Borden when Mrs. Borden talked with her.

Q. Did you hear them talking on Thursday morning?

A. Yes. Mrs. Borden asked some questions and Miss Lizzie answered very civilized, but I don't know what they were talking about.

Q. Do you think there was any trouble in the family that morning?

A. No, sir, I didn't see any trouble.

Q. When you came in from the yard, what did you do about the screen door?

A. I hooked it.

Sullivan's testimony from the inquest had been submitted as evidence. Written records are kept of testimony at inquests and preliminary hearings. These records can be read into the trial record.

Once the judge accepts testimony as part of the record, it can be referred to during a trial. These records are often used to point out inconsistencies in a witness's testimony. At the inquest Sullivan had testified that she didn't know if she had hooked the screen door or not.

The defense wanted to show this contradictory evidence to support its theory that an unknown assailant had sneaked into the house.

Q. Are you sure you hooked the screen door? At the inquest you said you didn't know whether you hooked it.

A. I guess I don't know whether I did or not. But it's likely I did, because it was always kept locked.

Q. Could someone go in and out the screen door without your hearing it?

A. Yes, sir, very easily.

Q. When you were talking with Mrs. Kelly's girl, could someone have walked in the unlocked screen door without your seeing him?

A. Of course.

Q. When you were outside washing the front windows, could you see someone go in the side door?

A. Anybody could come in from the backyard, but not from the front.

Q. When you were talking with Mrs. Kelly's girl, could you see the front gate or the side gate or the sidewalk?

A. No, sir.

The defense suggested why Bridget didn't know about the note:

Q. Could somebody have brought a note without your knowing it?

A. Well, if they came to the front door I wouldn't know, but if they came to the back door I would know.

Q. But they wouldn't necessarily go to the back door, would they? So you can't say that a note didn't come?

A. No, sir.

The closing questions focused on Lizzie's clothes.

Q. When Miss Borden was on the sofa in the dining room, did you see any blood on her?

A. None at all. Nothing on her clothing or her face or hands or anywhere.

Q. Do you remember what dress she wore?

A. No, sir.

Be the Jury

Could someone have sneaked past Bridget into the house?

How could Lizzie be the murderer if her clothing showed no blood?

Thursday, June 8, 1893

For the first time since the trial began, the weather was cool. Gentle breezes floated through the courtroom after three blistering hot days.

Witness: **Dr. Seabury W. Bowen**

Direct Examination by the Prosecution

Bowen had been the Borden family doctor and friend for twenty-six years. He lived diagonally across the street from them.

Q. Please tell us what you saw at 11:30 A.M.
A. Mr. Borden was lying on the sitting-room sofa. His coat was folded up on a cushion. There was blood everywhere, on the carpet, on the wall over the sofa, even on a picture hanging on the wall. His face was covered with blood. The blood was still fresh. He was very badly cut, apparently with a sharp instrument. His face was unrecognizable as human. I felt his pulse and knew he was dead.

The prosecutor showed the official photograph of Mr. Borden's body to the witness and then to the jury.

I went back to the kitchen and asked Lizzie if she had seen anyone. She said she hadn't. Then I asked her, "Where have you been?" She replied, "In the barn looking for some iron."

Q. Did anyone ask about Mrs. Borden?

A. Not until Lizzie asked me to telegraph her sister, who was away visiting friends. Then I asked, "Where is Mrs. Borden?" Lizzie said that Mrs. Borden had received a note from a sick friend and had gone out. When I returned from sending the telegram, Mrs. Churchill told me that Mrs. Borden was dead upstairs.

I went up to the guest room. Mrs. Borden was lying facedown in a pool of dark, congealed blood. She had been struck on the head and the nape of the neck many times. There was no sign of a struggle. I placed my hand on her head, then felt her pulse. She was dead.

The prosecutor pressed Bowen to describe Lizzie's dress, hoping to prove that she had lied when she said she had worn a dark-blue silk dress.

Q. What did Miss Borden wear that morning?

A. The only time I noticed her clothing was after she went up to her room. She came down wearing a different dress. It was a pink dress.

Q. Did you notice anything about the dress she had on before?

A. It was an ordinary, unattractive, common dress. But I didn't notice it specifically.

The prosecutor held up Lizzie's shiny dark-blue heavy silk dress that she had said she had worn that day.

Q. Is this the dress she wore that morning?

A. I don't know.

Q. At the inquest you said her dress was a "sort of drab, not-much-color-to-it dress, a morning cotton dress." Is this the dress?

A. I don't know.

Q. What color do you call this dress?

A. Dark blue.

Cross-Examination by the Defense

Q. You knew that Mrs. Borden was lying on the floor of the guest room. When you went up the stairs, did you see her?

A. No. I didn't see her until I was at the guest-room door.

Be the Jury

Why did Lizzie change her dress?

If neither Kiernan nor Bowen saw anything going up the stairs, why should Lizzie have?

Witness: **Adelaide Churchill**
Direct Examination by the Prosecution

Churchill, a neighbor, saw Lizzie shortly after the murders.

Q. Why did you go over to the Bordens' that morning?

A. I saw Bridget walking quickly from Dr. Bowen's house to the Borden house. She looked very white. I thought someone was sick. I saw Lizzie standing inside the kitchen screen door. I opened my window and asked her what was the matter. She replied, "Oh, Mrs. Churchill, do come over. Someone has killed Father."

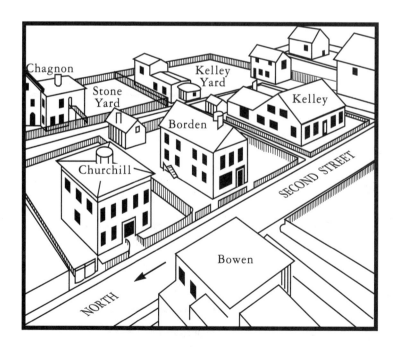

I went over. Lizzie was sitting on a stair. I put my hand on her and said, "Oh, Lizzie! Where is your father?" She answered, "In the sitting room." Then I asked, "Where were you when it happened?" She said she was in the barn getting a piece of iron.

"Where is your mother?" I asked. She said, "I don't know. She got a note from someone who is sick. But I don't know who. But I think she is killed, too, for I thought I heard her come in."

Then we went into the dining room. Lizzie lay down on the sofa. I fanned her. Then I went upstairs with Bridget to see if Mrs. Borden had come back. Going up the stairs, we saw part of a woman's body on the floor of the guest room. Bridget ran downstairs immediately. I walked down right after.

Q. What kind of dress was the prisoner wearing?

A. A light-blue cotton dress with a navy-blue diamond figure on it.

The prosecutor held up the blue silk dress again.

Q. Was this the dress?

A. I didn't see her wear it that morning.

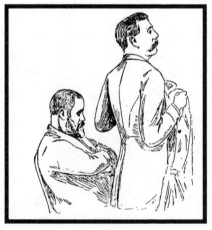

Sketch from *The New York Recorder*

Cross-Examination by the Defense

Again the defense zeroed in on how Lizzie looked shortly after the murders:

Q. When you first saw Miss Lizzie, did you see any blood on her dress?

A. No sir.

Q. When you fanned her, did you see any blood on her dress, or her hands, or her face?

A. No, sir.

Q. Was her hair disarranged?

A. No, sir.

Q. What about her shoes?

A. I didn't notice them at all.

Be the Jury

If Lizzie didn't wear that navy-blue dress that morning, why did she lie, and where is the dress she wore?

Witness: **Alice M. Russell**

When Russell's name was called, Lizzie, who had been staring into space and playing with her fan, looked up. Her body tensed. Her eyes followed Russell up to the witness box and never left her face during Russell's testimony. Russell had been a friend of Emma's and Lizzie's for many years, but she had not talked with either sister since agreeing to testify as a witness for the state.

Direct Examination by the Prosecution

The prosecutor tried to show that Lizzie's conversation with Russell established that she was plotting the murders.

Q. Describe your talk with the prisoner the night before the murders.
A. She said that she was going to visit a friend in Marion. She said she felt depressed. She had a terrible feeling something bad was going to happen. Everyone but Bridget had gotten sick the night before. She thought it was from baker's bread because Bridget didn't eat it. I told her, "If it had been the bread, other people in town would have gotten sick, too." She said, "I guess so but sometimes I think our milk might be poisoned." She said Mrs. Borden thought it had been poisoned.

Then she said she was afraid someone would harm her father because he was so rude to people. A man had come to see him. Her father had ordered him out of the house. She also said she saw a man run around the house one night.

Then she told me the barn had been broken into twice. She also told me that somebody had broken into the house in May in broad daylight when she and Emma and Bridget were in the house. They didn't hear anything. Things were stolen from Mrs. Borden's dressing room. I was surprised. Neither she nor Emma had ever told me about this robbery. Lizzie said her father forbade them to talk about it.

Q. Where did Lizzie say she had been when her father was killed?

A. In the barn looking for a piece of tin or iron to fix up her screen.

Q. Can you describe her dress that morning?

A. No, not at all. But I do remember that when she went upstairs, she changed into a pink-and-white striped housedress.

Next Russell explained that Lizzie had burned a dress that she might have worn the morning of the murders. The prosecutor believed this was more proof of her guilt.

Q. What happened on Sunday?

A. I went into the kitchen. Miss Emma was at the sink. Miss Lizzie was at the stove with a skirt in her hand. Miss Emma said, "What are you going to do?" Lizzie said, "I'm going to burn this old thing. It's covered with paint." I left the room without saying anything. Later I saw Miss Lizzie in the kitchen ripping part of the dress. I told her that she shouldn't let anybody see her do that. She didn't answer. I left the room.

Q. Did you ever say anything else to her about it?

A. Yes, on Monday morning, I told her that I thought that burning the dress was the worst thing she could have done. She said, "Then why did you let me do it? Why didn't you tell me?"

Q. One last item. Miss Russell, what kind of a dress did she burn?

A. It was a light-blue cotton dress with a small dark diamond figure on it.

Cross-Examination by the Defense

The defense reinforced the fact that no one had seen any blood on Lizzie or her clothes.

Q. Can you tell us anything about the dress Lizzie wore that morning?

A. No, sir.

Q. Did you see any blood on her clothing or her face?

A. No, sir.

Q. Was her hair disturbed?

A. I don't think it was. I would have noticed it if it was.

Q. Did you see any blood on the dress she burned?

A. No, but I didn't examine it closely. I did see that the edge of the dress was soiled.

Be the Jury

Why did Lizzie burn her light-blue dress?

Had Lizzie worn that light-blue dress the morning of the murders?

If Lizzie was the murderer, why didn't anyone see blood on her?

Friday, June 9, 1893

On this morning, as on every morning of the trial so far, there was a scramble for seats. Every day, the reporters listened attentively, and then rushed to wire the day's events to their newsrooms. Artists from daily papers and weeklies sketched the lawyers, the judges, the spectators, and witnesses.

All eyes were on Lizzie as she entered the courtroom. She was always escorted by one or more ministers from Fall River. She was always dressed in black, the color of mourning. She seemed to take no notice of the reporters.

Sketch from the *New York Daily Tribune*

Witness: **John Fleet**
Direct Examination by the Prosecution

John Fleet, assistant city marshall of Fall River, arrived at the Borden house at 11:45 A.M. The prosecutor believed Lizzie's remarks to him just after the murders revealed her hostile feelings about her stepmother:

Q. Please describe your interview with the prisoner.
A. I asked her if she had any idea who could have killed her father and mother. She said, "She is not my mother, sir. She is my stepmother. My mother died when I was a child." I asked her if she knew anything about the murders. She said she didn't. All she knew was that her father came home about 10:30 or 10:45 A.M. and he looked feeble. He went into the sitting room. She suggested he lie down on the sofa. She went into the dining room to finish ironing some handkerchiefs. Then she went out to the barn. She stayed up in the loft about a half hour. When she came back to the house, she found him dead. I asked her if she thought Miss Sullivan could have been the killer. She said "No."

I asked if there had been anyone suspicious around the house this morning. She said that about 9 A.M. she saw a man talking with her father at the front door. She didn't hear what they were talking about, but the man spoke like an Englishman.

The prosecutor zeroed in on the broken hatchet, which he believed was the murder weapon. He believed Lizzie had broken the hatchet, washed it, then rolled the blade in ashes to destroy any trace of blood.

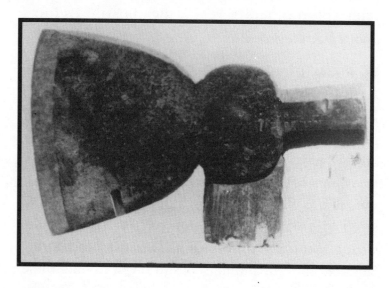

Q. Please describe the handleless hatchet that you found in the cellar.

A. It was in a box with other tools on a shelf on the fireplace. The head had been broken off from the handle. It was a new break. The wood around the break wasn't dark, as it would have been if the break happened a while ago. The blade was covered with heavy dust or what I thought were white ashes on both sides.

Q. Was there dust on the other tools?

A. Yes, but that dust was lighter and finer than the dust on this hatchet.

Q. Did you see any ashes on the wood where the hatchet was broken?

A. Yes, there were ashes there, too.

Cross-Examination by the Defense

The defense hoped to suggest that the hatchet had become covered with ashes because the cellar was so filled with ashes that they simply settled on the blade as dust would.

Q. Were there any other ashes in the room?

A. Yes, there was a pile of ashes on the cellar floor where Mr. Borden dumped the ashes from the furnace. The pile was only a few feet away from the shelf where I found the box. It was a big pile. The ashes could have filled at least a fifty-bushel basket.

Q. Were either of the other two hatchets covered with ashes?

A. The small one was somewhat dusty.

Q. Is it possible that the dust might have come from this pile of ashes?

A. Yes, it's possible.

Be the Jury

Wasn't Lizzie's comment about her stepmother rather mean considering she had just been murdered?

Could Lizzie have rolled the hatchet in ashes to make it look dusty?

Witness: **Officer Philip Harrington**

Direct Examination by the Prosecution

Harrington arrived at the house about 12:15 P.M. Lizzie gave him a different version of her whereabouts when her father was being murdered from what she had told Sullivan or Bowen.

Q. Where did the prisoner say she had been when her father was murdered?

A. She said she had been in the barn for twenty minutes. I asked, "Isn't it hard to be so accurate about the time?" She insisted she was there for twenty minutes. I asked if she had seen anybody in or around the yard or anybody coming down the street when she went to and from the barn. She said no. I asked if she had heard any noise like someone walking or closing a screen door. She said she couldn't hear anything because she was up in the barn loft. Then she said that a few weeks ago her father had angry words with a man. She couldn't remember much more about the man. I said, "Owing to the atrociousness of this crime, perhaps you are not in a mental condition to give as clear a statement of the facts as you will be tomorrow." She made a stiff curtsy and said, "No, I can tell you all I know now just as well as at any other time."

Q. During any part of the interview was she in tears or did her voice break?

A. No, sir.

Q. Please describe your interview with Bridget Sullivan.

A. She was so upset that she couldn't talk straight.

Q. What was the temperature in the barn that day?

A. Extremely hot.

Q. Were the windows open?

A. No, they were closed.

Q. Later, in the kitchen, what did you see?

A. Dr. Bowen threw some scraps of paper into the stove. I saw the name "Emma" on one of the scraps of paper. I also saw some burned paper, about twelve inches long and two inches wide, rolled up in a cylinder, in the stove.

The burned paper offered a possible connection—the paper was the same length as the handle of the broken hatchet.

Cross-Examination by the Defense

Q. You saw the name Emma on one of these scraps. Was there any attempt by Dr. Bowen to withhold the paper?

A. No, sir.

Q. At the inquest, you testified that at least one window of the barn loft was open. Today you testified that all windows were closed. Which is correct?

Harrington hesitated.

A. I was correct at the inquest. I remember a window being open.

Be the Jury

Why was Lizzie so calm after these ghastly murders?

What was that scrap of paper?

Could Lizzie have put the broken handle inside the roll of paper and burned it in the stove?

Witness: **Officer Michael Mullaly**

Direct Examination by the Prosecution

Mullaly arrived at the Borden house at 11:37 A.M. Lizzie told him another story of her whereabouts during the murder.

Q. Where did the prisoner say she had been when her father was murdered?

A. In the barn loft, eating some pears and looking over some lead for sinkers [weights for fishing lines]. She heard a peculiar noise, something like scraping. So she came back to the house.

Q. What else did you do at the Borden house?

A. I went to the cellar, where I found a box with two hatchets and two axes. Then I searched the yard, the woodpile, the upper and lower parts of the barn, and then the guest room. Then I went back to the cellar. Mr. Fleet was there examining a hatchet without a handle. The break looked fresh, as if it was just broken. Both sides of the blade were covered with ashes. It looked as though the ashes were wiped on.

Cross-Examination by the Defense

The defense sought confirmation that the police search was so thorough that if Lizzie had had bloody clothes, they would have been found.

Q. Did you find any weapon or any indication of blood on any part of the premises on the outside of the house?

A. No.

Q. Did you make a pretty thorough search outdoors?

A. As far as I know, I did.

Be the Jury

Why did Lizzie tell different stories about where she had been?

Could Lizzie hear a scraping noise all the way up in the barn loft?

Saturday, June 10, 1893

Witness: Officer William Medley
Direct Examination by the Prosecution

The prosecutor believed that Medley's testimony destroyed Lizzie's alibi. Medley examined the barn around 11:43 A.M.

Q. What did you see in the barn?
A. I went upstairs to the loft. When I reached four steps from the top, I looked around. There was hay dust and other dust on the floor. Nothing looked disturbed. I stooped down and looked across the floor to see if there were any marks on it. I didn't see any. I put my hand down on the floor to see if I could make an impression. I did. Then I stepped up on the top stair and took four or five steps on the edge of the barn floor. I stooped down and looked eye level with the floor to see if I could see my footprints. I saw them clearly. But I didn't see any other footprints in the dust.
Q. What was the temperature in the barn?
A. Hot, very hot.
Q. Were the windows open or closed?
A. Closed.

Cross-Examination by the Defense

The defense wanted to show that Medley had not carefully searched the barn.

Q. Did any of the windows have curtains?

A. I don't remember. But I think there was a curtain on one window.

Q. Did you look at boxes or baskets up there?

A. I didn't go on the floor other than what I described. I just stood and looked around. But I did see a bench on the south side of the barn with things on it. I don't know what they were.

Q. Did you go round on the barn floor?

A. No, sir, I did not.

Q. Is it correct to say that you stood and looked about for two or three minutes?

A. Yes, sir.

Be the Jury

Was Medley's examination thorough enough to prove that Lizzie hadn't been in the barn?

Is it believable that anyone would spend twenty or thirty minutes in a barn loft, with the windows shut, on a hundred-degree day?

If Lizzie was up in the barn loft, why weren't there any footprints?

Monday, June 12, 1893

The prosecution asked to submit Lizzie's inquest testimony into the record. The defense did not want the jury to hear what she had said at the inquest, so the defense exercised its right to *object* to having the testimony admitted. The defense insisted this evidence was *inadmissible*—inappropriate because it didn't fall within the rules of the law.

When judges *sustain* (support) the objection, evidence is not presented. If the objection is *overruled*, evidence is admitted.

The Chief Justice sent the jury out of the courtroom while the two lawyers argued. After listening to both sides, the judges decided not to admit the testimony. When Lizzie heard the decision, she covered her eyes with her handkerchief and cried. The jury was brought back into the courtroom.

Witness: **Dr. William Dolan**

Direct Examination by the Prosecution

Medical examiner Dolan was one of three medical experts who performed autopsies on the bodies. In an autopsy, a body is examined after death to discover how and when the person died.

Sketch from *The New York Recorder*

Dolan was given a plaster cast formed from Mr. Borden's skull. Using a blue crayon, he outlined each of the ten blows that had killed Mr. Borden. He described the wounds and how blood must have spurted from the corpse.

A juror, overwhelmed by the details,

fainted. Chief Justice Mason called an emergency recess. After the recess, Dolan resumed his testimony. The prosecutor wanted to show that Lizzie had the strength to commit the crimes.

Q. What did you conclude from your autopsy of Mr. Borden?

A. That the wounds in the head caused the death. There were no wounds except those on his head.

Q. Could Mr. Borden's wounds have been struck with a hatchet by a woman of ordinary strength?

A. Yes, sir.

Q. Considering the condition of the victims' blood, the heat of their bodies, and the contents of their stomachs, how much time elapsed between their deaths?

A. Mrs. Borden died first, about one and a half hours to two hours before her husband.

Tuesday, June 13, 1893
Cross-Examination by the Defense

The defense questioned Dolan about the spattering of blood from the repeated blows.

Q. When a hatchet goes into a wound, does its blade get covered with blood, particularly on the edge?

A. Yes, sir.

Q. Do you think it was probable that the assailant would be covered with blood or at least spattered?

A. Yes, sir; there would be spatters.

Q. Where would these spatters be from murdering Mr. Borden?

A. On the assailant's chest and head area and probably on his hands.

Q. If the assailant stood over Mrs. Borden's body, would there be a general spattering of blood over the assailant's body?

A. I don't know whether there would be a general spattering over the entire body. But I think there would surely be some on the lower part of the body.

Be the Jury

If Lizzie was the murderer, how could she have avoided being spattered?

Witness: **Dr. Edward S. Wood**
Direct Examination by the Prosecution

Dr. Wood was a toxicologist, an expert in poisons and bloodstains. He had examined the hatchet and Lizzie's clothing.

Q. Was there any blood on the prisoner's clothes?

A. There was no blood on her clothes, shoes, or stockings, except for a spot as large as the size of the head of a small pin on the outside of her white petticoat.

Q. Was there blood on the handleless hatchet?

A. No. My tests showed it absolutely free of blood.

Q. Could blood have been washed off it so it couldn't be detected?

A. Absolutely, if the weapon was very thoroughly washed with cold water. But it couldn't be done by a careless washing. The broken hatchet would have to be washed before the handle was broken. Because it would be almost impossible to quickly wash blood off that broken end.

Q. Please describe the handleless hatchet.

A. The head was broken off from the handle. There was a white film, like ashes, over both sides of the blade. There were more ashes in the middle of the blade.

Cross-Examination by the Defense

The handleless hatchet was shown to Wood:

Q. Can you tell when this hatchet was broken?
A. I have no opinion as to the freshness of the break.

The defense posed an explanation for the tiny spot of blood on Lizzie's slip:

Q. You said that the outside of Miss Borden's petticoat had a spot of blood on it. Can you positively say that this spot was not menstrual blood?
A. No, sir, I cannot.
Q. It could be, then?
A. Yes, sir, it could be.

Be the Jury

Could Lizzie have washed the hatchet and the broken handle, wrapped the handle in the paper cylinder and burned it in the kitchen stove?

Wouldn't menstrual blood be on the inside of a petticoat instead of, or as well as, on the outside?

Witness: **Dr. Frank W. Draper**
Direct Examination by the Prosecution

Draper was the medical examiner for the city of Boston. He explained that the cutting edge of the handleless hatchet was three and a half inches. He had determined that from looking at Mr. Borden's skull.

A large package was brought into the courtroom. The prosecutor unwrapped it, and lifted up the fleshless skull of Mr. Borden. Gasps and cries were heard in the courtroom. Lizzie fainted.

A magazine illustration showed Lizzie fainting in the courtroom.

When Lizzie had revived, she was taken out of the room, and Draper resumed his testimony. Then Draper, with the help of Dr. Cheever, another medical expert, demonstrated how the blade of the handleless hatchet fit into all the wound marks on the skull.

Q. Do you think this handleless hatchet could have made those wounds?
A. Yes.
Q. Do you think a woman of ordinary strength could have made these wounds with an ordinary hatchet?
A. Yes.

Cross-Examination by the Defense

Q. You said the murder weapon had a three-and-a-half-inch edge. Is that exact?
A. Well, the weapon could have had an edge of two and three quarters or three inches. But I think three and a half is more accurate.
Q. Could blood be so removed from a metal instrument that your test would find no trace of it?
A. Yes, but it could not easily be done.

Again the defense pointed out that there would have been blood on the murderer.

Q. In your opinion, would the assailant be spattered with blood?

A. Yes. With a great deal of blood.

Q. Is it easy to get blood out of one's hair?

A. It is almost impossible. You have to shampoo the hair thoroughly.

The defense produced a hatchet that was the same size as the handleless hatchet. Dr. Draper was asked to fit its blade into the wounds in Mr. Borden's skull as he had done with the blade of the other hatchet. The blade didn't fit.

Redirect by the Prosecution

The prosecutor wanted to clear up the misleading testimony about the weapon that had come out of the cross-examination. He asked Draper to explain why the second hatchet didn't fit the indentations on the skull even though it was the same size.

Q. Would all hatchets with a cutting edge of three and a half inches fit the wounds?

A. No, sir, only a hatchet with an edge that accurately applies itself to that wound in the bones.

Q. In your opinion, could these wounds have been inflicted by this broken hatchet?

A. Yes.

Q. If the hatchet had been used around 9:30 A.M., immediately cleaned with water, and then used again at 11 A.M., could the blood be removed so that it would not be detected by chemical analysis?
A. Yes.

The prosecutor offered a simple explanation why Lizzie's clothing was free of blood.

Q. Is there a garment worn during surgery that protects clothing from blood spattering?
A. Yes, sir.
Q. Is it easily put on and easily taken off?
A. Yes. It's quickly changed after every operation.

Be the Jury

If Lizzie wore an outer garment, wouldn't that explain why she had no blood on her clothes?

Could Lizzie also have covered her hair?

How can the handleless hatchet not be the weapon if it fits so perfectly into the wounds?

Did Lizzie have enough time to wash the blade after the second murder?

Everyone turned to look at Lizzie as she reentered the courtroom and sat down at the table with her lawyers.

Wednesday, June 14, 1893
Witness: Anna H. Gifford
Direct Examination by the Prosecution

Mrs. Gifford, a dressmaker, had sewn clothes for the Bordens for seven years. The prosecutor believed her testimony proved Lizzie hated her stepmother.

Q. What happened last March first?
A. I was sewing for Miss Borden and I said something about her mother. And she said, "Don't call her my mother. She's a mean old thing, a good-for-nothing." I said, "You don't mean that." And she said, "Yes, I don't have much to do with her. I stay in my room most of the time." I asked, "You come down for meals, don't you?" And she said, "We don't eat with them if we can help it."

During Mrs. Gifford's testimony Lizzie's face became red. The cross-examination of Mrs. Gifford by the defense developed no new information. The defense did not shake her firm recollection of her talk with Lizzie.

Be the Jury

Is there enough evidence to show that Lizzie's hatred of her stepmother could be a motive?

The prosecutor wanted to cast doubt on the defense's "unknown assailant" theory. He called five witnesses to show that no strangers had been seen escaping from the Borden house.

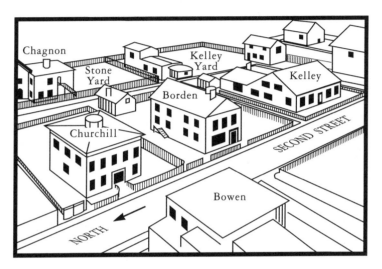

Witness: **Lucy Collet**

Collet worked at Dr. Chagnon's house, answering his phone and receiving office callers. She arrived at Chagnon's house at 10:45 A.M. on August fourth and found the doors locked. So she stayed out on the porch, near the front steps on the left side facing the yard, between the steps and the passageway leading to the Borden barn.

Direct Examination by the Prosecution

Q. How long were you there?

A. From 10:45 until some time after 11.

Q. During all that time did you ever see anyone pass out of the Chagnon yard?

A. No.

Cross-Examination by the Defense

Q. Were you looking at every moment, so you would have seen if anyone had come through the yard?

A. No, I wasn't particularly looking.

Q. Did anyone come to see the doctor?

A. Yes, one man.

Q. Do you know who he was?

A. Yes. He was Mr. Robinson, one of the defense lawyers.

Robinson and the other two defense lawyers laughed.

Be the Jury

If there was an unknown assailant, why wasn't there any blood in the hallways or the closets where that person must have hidden between the murders?

Witness: **Thomas Bolles**
Direct Examination by the Prosecution

Bolles had been washing a carriage in Mrs. Chagnon's yard that morning.

Q. Could you see into the Borden yard?
A. Yes, I could see the well house in that yard.
Q. Did you see anybody come in or out of that yard?
A. No.

Cross-Examination by the Defense

Q. Could you see the whole Borden yard?
A. No, the barn, the well house, and a big piece of latticework got in the way of seeing everything.

Witnesses: **Patrick McGowan, Joseph Desrosier and John Denny**

These men worked in a stone yard behind the Bordens' yard. All three men testified that they hadn't seen anybody leaving the Borden house by that route.

Be the Jury

If there was an unknown assailant, why didn't anyone see that person leave the Borden house?

Witness: **Hannah Reagan**
Direct Examination by the Prosecution

Reagan, the matron at the Fall River police station, told of an angry exchange between Emma and Lizzie.

Q. What happened between Miss Lizzie Borden and her sister on August twenty-four?

A. Miss Emma came to visit her sister, as she did every day. I was in another room four feet away. I heard very loud talk. I came to my door. Miss Lizzie was lying on her left side. Her sister was bent right over her. Miss Lizzie said, "Emma, you have given me away, haven't you?" Miss Emma said, "No, Lizzie, I have not." "You have," Lizzie said, "But I won't give in one inch." Miss Lizzie sat up and put up her finger over her mouth to indicate they should stop talking. I was standing in the doorway.

Then Miss Lizzie lay down on the couch and closed her eyes. Miss Emma sat right down beside her. They sat there till their lawyer came at 11 A.M. Miss Lizzie didn't speak to her sister or turn her face to her all that time. When Miss Emma left, she didn't say good-bye to her sister.

Cross-Examination by the Defense

The defense needed to show that Reagan lied about the quarrel to discredit her testimony:

Q. Did Miss Borden come again that day to visit her sister?
A. Yes, in the afternoon.
Q. You speak of the talk as a quarrel?
A. Yes.
Q. You told this story about this so-called quarrel to a reporter. The story was printed in the newspaper. Do you remember what the story said?
A. No, sir.

The defense named the person who would appear later and testify that Mrs. Reagan had lied:

Q. Did you tell Thomas Hickey that the newspaper story wasn't true?
A. No, sir, I did not.

Be the Jury

What did Lizzie mean by: "Emma, you have given me away"?

Witness: **Eli Bence**

Direct Examination by the Prosecution

Q. Where do you work?

A. I am a drug clerk at D. R. Smith's Pharmacy in Fall River.

Q. How long have you worked there?

A. Four and a half years.

The defense rose and objected to Bence's testimony. The Chief Justice called both lawyers to the bench. They talked for a few minutes; then the Chief Justice asked the jury to leave the courtroom.

After listening to the lawyers' arguments the judges decided not to admit Bence's testimony. The jury was brought back into the room.

The prosecution rested its case.

The Defense's Opening Statement

Thursday, June 15, 1883

The defense opened its case. Andrew Jennings had been Andrew Borden's lawyer. He had served as a representative in the state house and as a state senator. Jennings was known as a powerful debater and speaker. This is his opening statement:

A young woman, who led an honorable, spotless life, has been accused of a crime that has shocked the world. You do not have to decide how this brutal deed was done or who did it. All you must decide is whether it can be proven beyond a reasonable doubt that Lizzie Borden is guilty. If you cannot do that, you cannot take her life.

There is not one bit of direct evidence against her. There is no weapon connected with her. There was not a spot of blood on her clothes, or person. The evidence against her is circumstantial. Circumstantial evidence is dangerous and misleading.

The facts in a case are links in a chain. Every link must be proved beyond a reasonable doubt. You cannot have the chain tied together by weak links and strong links. You cannot take certain facts which you believe and tie them to other facts that you reasonably doubt. You must throw aside every fact that you reasonably doubt. And unless, with the links left, you can tie this defendant to the murders, you must acquit her.

In analyzing the evidence, you must think about four things—weapon, motive, sole opportunity, and conduct and appearance of the defendant. The government has not produced a weapon or a motive. There was nothing between the defendant and her father that would cause her to do this wicked, wicked act. Even if the prosecutor shows a motive for her to kill her stepmother, she had absolutely no motive to kill her father.

And was Miss Lizzie the only person who could have committed the crime? No. The prosecutor has not produced one living soul who saw Mr. Borden leave his house in the morning and go to the bank. If Mr. Borden could be invisible, isn't it possible for somebody else to escape from this same house and walk quietly away?

I ask you to listen carefully to the evidence. You will learn that there were strangers seen about the Borden house—they had the opportunity to commit the murders. These strangers have not yet been found. We shall show you that the government's claim about Miss Lizzie's not being in the barn is false. As for the burned dress, Miss Lizzie did burn it—in broad daylight with witnesses and police all around.

After you hear all the evidence, you must decide whether the government has satisfactorily proved beyond a reasonable doubt that the defendant killed not only her stepmother, but her loved and loving father.

All through Jennings's speech, Lizzie had covered her face with her handkerchief to hide her crying.

The Defense's Strategy

In trying to prove Lizzie not guilty beyond a reasonable doubt, the defense will present evidence to cast further doubt on damaging testimony given by prosecution witnesses. In addition, the defense will offer other theories to establish:

- the *possibility* of an unknown assailant;
- Lizzie's *alibi;*
- reasonable *explanations* for Lizzie's behavior after the murders.

The Prosecution's Strategy

The prosecutor will cross-examine the defense's witnesses and try to cast doubt on their believability and their accounts of the events.

Defense Witnesses

Sketch from *The New York Recorder*

The courtroom was packed as it had been every day of the trial. The defense had three witnesses who would testify about unidentified persons seen near Second Street the day of the murders. The defense hoped this testimony strengthened the idea of an unknown assassin and cast doubt on Lizzie's sole opportunity to commit the murders.

Witness: **Mark Chase**
Direct Examination by the Defense

Chase worked in a stable right opposite the Kellys on Second Street. He had seen a carriage parked north of the Borden house farther up the hill at 11 A.M. the day of the murders.

Q. Could you describe the man in the carriage?
A. His back was to me. He was sitting in the open buggy with a brown hat and black coat.
Q. Had you ever seen him before?
A. No, sir.

Cross-Examination by the Prosecution

Q. How much of the man did you see?
A. From his shoulder up to the top of his head.
Q. Did you see any part of his face?
A. Yes, the side.
Q. Did the man ever turn around?
A. No.

Witness: **Benjamin Handy**
Direct Examination by the Defense

Handy had been a doctor in Fall River for twenty years. He had passed by the Borden house in his carriage on August fourth at 9 A.M. and again a little after 10:30 A.M.

Q. Did you see anything when you passed by the Borden house the day of the murders?

A. Yes, I saw a young man about thirty years old. He was about five feet, five inches tall and weighed about one hundred thirty-five pounds. He had a very pale complexion, paler than common. His eyes were fixed on the sidewalk. He wore a light suit of clothes, a collar and necktie.

Q. Had you ever seen him before?

A. I had a faint idea that I had seen him on Second Street a few days before.

Cross-Examination by the Prosecution

Q. How was the man walking?

A. Very slowly, like he was scarcely moving.

Q. Did he look drunk?

A. No. He seemed agitated or weak or confused.

Be the Jury

Could one of these men be the murderer?

Witness: **Herman Lubinsky**
Direct Examination by the Defense

Lubinsky was an ice-cream peddler. The defense believed that his testimony proved that Lizzie had been in the barn at the time her father was murdered.

Q. What did you see when you drove by the Borden house on August fourth?

A. A few minutes after 11, I saw a lady come out of the way from the barn right to the back of the Borden house. She wore a dark dress. She had nothing on her head. And she was walking very slowly.

Q. How do you know it was a few minutes after 11?

A. I was late that morning and worried about it, so I looked at my watch as I left the stable.

Q. Did you see the woman go into the house?

A. No.

Q. Did you recognize this woman?

A. No.

Q. Are you sure she wasn't Bridget Sullivan?

A. Yes. I delivered ice cream to that house three weeks before and I met Miss Sullivan then. It wasn't her.

Cross-Examination by the Prosecution

The prosecutor tried to confuse Lubinsky to prove he was not a dependable witness.

Q. How much after 11 did you look at your watch?
A. I can't say.
Q. Did you actually see the woman leave the barn?
A. No.
Q. Did you actually see her go into the house?
A. No. I saw her about two or three feet from the kitchen door.
Q. Why were you looking around?
A. Because I like to look around.
Q. Do you go down that street every day?
A. Yes, every day.
Q. But you didn't take any notice any other day?
A. Something made me look at it that day. What has a person got eyes for, but to look with?

Be the Jury

Was Lizzie the woman Lubinsky saw?

If he was wrong about the time, could the woman have been Adelaide Churchill or Alice Russell?

Witness: **Charles E. Gardiner**
Direct Examination by the Defense

Gardiner owned the stable where Lubinsky kept his horse. His testimony was crucial to establishing whether Lubinsky had passed the Borden house when Lizzie said she came from the barn.

Q. What time did Mr. Lubinsky leave your stables on August fourth?

A. Between 11:05 and 11:10 A.M.

Q. How can you be sure of the time?

A. Because the horses are always fed at 11. Lubinsky arrived before they were finished eating, so I looked at my watch. It was 11:08 A.M.

Q. Was he concerned about the time?

A. Yes, he kept yelling to me to hurry up. He had a job to drive a traveling salesman around and he didn't want to be late.

Cross-Examination by the Prosecution

The prosecutor tried to shake Gardiner's memory of the time.

Q. Did you pass by the Borden house that morning?

A. Yes, I left the stables about fifteen minutes after Mr. Lubinsky left.

Q. And when did you arrive near the Borden house?

A. About 11:30 A.M.

Q. Did you see anybody or anything?

A. No, there was no activity going on.

Q. Are you sure of the time? By 11:30 there were many people around.

A. I'm sure.

Q. And you say that there was no activity going on?

A. Yes.

Be the Jury

How could Mr. Gardiner have passed the house at 11:30 and not seen anybody when there were people there by then?

If Gardiner is wrong about the time he passed by the Borden house, is he right about the time Lubinsky left the stable?

Witness: **Everett Brown**
Direct Examination by the Defense

Teenagers Everett Brown and Thomas Barlow claimed they were in the barn loft before Officer Medley. If that was true, then Medley should have seen their footprints. The defense wanted to show that Medley's testimony was unreliable.

Q. Please tell us about August fourth.
A. Thomas Barlow and I left my house about 11:18 A.M. and went directly to the Borden house. We went into the yard. We tried to get into the house, but the police wouldn't let us in. So we went into the barn. We stood there for a few minutes. Barlow said he wouldn't go up to the loft. He was afraid someone might drop an ax on him. But we both went upstairs anyway. We looked out of the window on the west side and went over to where the hay was; we left after about five minutes.
Q. What did you do next?
A. We went back into the yard, then tried to peek into the southeast corner of the house, but we couldn't. I seen Officer Fleet coming up the walk. Then we all got put out of the yard.

Cross-Examination by the Prosecution

The prosecutor pressed Brown about the exact time that he had been in the barn to show what a poor witness he was.

Q. What time did you get there?

A. I can't say what time.

Q. Was it nearer 12 or 11?

A. I don't know the time.

Q. You don't know anything about the time?

A. No, sir.

Q. Did you see Officer Medley?

A. No, sir.

Q. How long did you hang around the Borden house?

A. Till about 10 that night.

Q. Did you ever see Officer Medley?

A. I might have seen him and I might not. I wasn't taking note of who I seen there.

Q. So he might have come in and gone out of the yard and you might not have seen him anyhow?

A. Yes, sir.

Witness: **Thomas Barlow**

Direct Examination by the Defense

Barlow echoed Brown's story. The defense hoped the testimony of the two boys discredited Medley's testimony.

Q. Tell us about going to the Borden house.

A. I got to Everett's house at 11 A.M. and I stayed there about eight minutes; then we went to the Borden house. We went in the side gate. We couldn't get into the house so we went into the barn and up to the loft.

Q. What was the temperature in the barn loft?

A. It was cooler in the barn than it was outdoors.

Cross-Examination by the Prosecution

The prosecutor tried to show that Barlow was a poor witness because it could not have been cool in the barn:

Q. Now did I understand you to say it was cooler up in the barn loft than it was anywhere else?
A. Yes, it was a cool place.
Q. What do you suppose made it so much cooler than the rest of the county?
A. I couldn't say. It's always warmer in the house than outdoors.

The prosecutor tried to show how child-like both boys were.

Q. Did you walk directly to the Borden house?
A. Well, we stopped sometimes. We were fooling along. He was pushing me off the sidewalk, and I was pushing him off.
Q. How long do you think it took, pushing him off the sidewalk and he pushing you back?
A. About ten or fifteen minutes.

The prosecutor concluded by trying to show that Brown's sense of time was vague and therefore unreliable.

Be the Jury

Are Brown and Barlow dependable witnesses?

Friday, June 16, 1893

Witness: Sarah Hart

Direct Examination by the Defense

Like Chase and Handy, Hart and her friend, Delia Manley, saw a stranger near the Borden house the day of the murders.

Q. Tell us what you saw at 9:50 A.M.

A. I was passing by the Borden house when I stopped to speak to my nephew. He was driving by in a carriage. I saw a young man standing at the Borden gateway. He leaned his elbow on the gatepost. He was there during the five minutes I was talking with my nephew.

Cross-Examination by the Prosecution

Q. Where was your nephew's carriage?

A. Between the Borden and Chagnon houses.

Q. So you couldn't see the man completely?

A. No, but there was nothing blocking my view when I was walking by.

Q. But you were talking to Mrs. Manley when you walked by?

A. Yes, of course.

Be the Jury

Did these strangers have enough time to commit the crimes?

What could their motive have been?

If a stranger was the murderer, wouldn't he or she have left the murder weapon in the house?

Witness: **Walter P. Stevens**
Direct Examination by the Defense

The defense hoped the testimony of the next two witnesses, Walter P. Stevens and Alfred Clarkson, would discredit Officer Medley's damaging testimony that he had seen no footprints in the barn. Stevens, a reporter for the Fall River *Daily News*, had been at the Fall River police station when the news of the murders came in, and he went directly to the Borden house.

Q. What did you do at the Borden house?

A. I went to the barn, walked around on the first floor, and then went up to the barn-loft floor. Then I went into the house.

Q. Did you see Officer Medley?

A. He wasn't there yet.

Q. Did you see him at all while you were at the Bordens' house?

A. I saw him coming down the street toward the house after I had been in the barn.

Cross-Examination by the Prosecution

Q. What time did you get to the Bordens'?

A. About noon.

Q. Are you absolutely sure that Officer Medley had not already been in the barn before you went there?

A. No, I'm not absolutely sure.

Witness: **Alfred C. Clarkson**
Direct Examination by the Defense

Newspaper reporter Clarkson said he arrived at the Borden premises at 11:38 A.M.

Q. What did you do at the Borden house?

A. I went into the barn and up into the loft.

Q. Did you see anybody else go into the barn?

A. Yes. Two other men went in.

Q. Did you see Officer Medley when you were on the Borden premises?

A. No.

Cross-Examination by the Prosecution

The prosecutor tried to get Clarkson to pinpoint the exact time he went into the barn.

Q. Did you look at your watch before you entered the barn?
A. No.
Q. Then how can you be sure it was 11:38?
A. I estimated it.
Q. Then you don't really know the exact time?
A. No.
Q. Is it possible that Officer Medley was around but that you didn't see him?
A. Yes, it's possible.

Be the Jury

Who was in the barn first: Stevens and Clarkson or Medley?

If Stevens and Clarkson were in the barn first, why didn't Medley see their footprints?

If Medley was in the barn first and didn't see any footprints, how could Lizzie have been there?

Witness: **Thomas Hickey**
Direct Examination by the Defense

The defense called Thomas Hickey to disprove Mrs. Reagan's testimony. Hickey was a reporter for the *Boston Herald*.

Q. Please describe your talk with Mrs. Reagan.

A. There was an article in the newspaper about a quarrel between Emma and Lizzie. Mrs. Reagan was the source of that article. The day after the article appeared, I went to see her at the jail. I said something like: "I see you are getting yourself in the papers." She laughed and said, "Yes, but I have got to take it back." After some other questions, I asked her if there had been a quarrel, and she said no. I asked her if she had told the reporter that Lizzie had said "You gave me away." She said she did not tell him that. Then I said, "Mrs. Reagan, is there any truth in the story that was printed?" And she said, "No, sir, no truth at all."

Cross-Examination by the Prosecution

The prosecutor tried to suggest that Hickey had a professional reason to discredit Mrs. Reagan's story.

Q. You represent the *Boston Herald*, and the story about this quarrel appeared in the *Boston Globe*. The two newspapers are rivals. When one gets an item of news that the other doesn't, it's considered a "scoop," isn't it?

A. Yes, sir.

Q. And in this particular instance, the *Globe* got a scoop on your paper?

A. Yes, sir.

Q. And of course, you wanted to show that the scoop was for nothing, wasn't it?

A. Well, yes.

Be the Jury

Why would Mrs. Reagan have lied?

Was she pressured to take back her story?

Witness: **Emma Borden**
Direct Examination by the Defense

Emma Borden was the defense's star witness. She was saved by the defense to be one of the last witnesses so that her testimony would be fresh in the jury's mind when it went out to decide the verdict. She produced bank books and stock certificates showing that Lizzie had $6,000 at the time of the murders. This was a large sum of money then, showing that Lizzie had more than enough for her needs. In the opening statement, the prosecutor had said Mr. Borden was rich, and the defense did not want the jury to think that Lizzie might have murdered her father for his money. Mr. Borden died without leaving a will, so his $300,000 estate would go automatically to his daughters.

The defense questioned Emma about a ring that Lizzie gave to her father that revealed their close bond.

Q. Did your father wear a ring?

A. Yes, sir. He received it from my sister Lizzie about ten or fifteen years ago. It had been her ring. He always wore it. It was the only jewelry he ever wore. It was on his finger when he was buried.

The defense shifted to the contents of the clothes closet on the second floor.

Q. When the police searched the clothes closet on Saturday afternoon, what was in it?

A. About eighteen dresses. All belonged to my sister and me except one that belonged to Mrs. Borden.

Q. How many of those dresses were blue or had blue in them?

A. Ten of them. Two were mine and seven were my sister's. One was my stepmother's.

Next Emma explained her role in the burning of the light-blue dress, contradicting Alice Russell's version of the incident.

Q. Please describe the cotton dress made for your sister in May.

A. It was a very cheap housedress. It was light-blue cotton with a darker diamond figure about an inch long and three quarters of an inch wide. It had a ruffle around the bottom. The ruffle was so long it sometimes dragged on the floor.

Q. Who made the dress?

A. Lizzie and I and our stepmother all worked on it with the dressmaker. It took us about two days.

Q. I understand the house was painted about two weeks after that. Did your sister get any paint on the dress then?

A. Yes. Along the front of the dress and on one side toward the bottom and some on the wrong side of the skirt.

Q. Did she wear the dress after the paint got on it?

A. Yes, she wore it until it got even more soiled.

Q. Where was that dress on the Saturday of the police search?

A. I saw it hanging in the clothes press over the front entry.

Q. What did you say to your sister about the dress?

A. I said, "You haven't destroyed that old dress yet. Why don't you?" It was very dirty and soiled and badly faded. So soiled and faded that it couldn't have been made over into anything else. The next morning, I was in the kitchen washing dishes. The windows and blinds were open. Police officers were in the yard. My sister was standing near the dining-room door. The dress was on her arm. She said, "I think I shall burn this old dress up." I said, "Why don't you," or "You had better," or "I would if I were you"—something like that. I can't remember the exact words.

Q. Miss Russell was in the kitchen too. Did she say anything about the dress?

A. Not then. But on Monday she told us she had told Mr. Hanscom, the detective we had hired, that all the dresses from the day of the murders were in the house. The fact that she had lied and not told him about the burned dress frightened me thoroughly. Lizzie and I told her to tell him that she had lied, and that we wanted her to correct the lie. She did.

Q. Did you hear Miss Russell say to your sister when she was burning the dress, "I wouldn't let anybody see me do that, Lizzie"?

A. I did not.

Next Emma contradicted Mrs. Reagan:

Q. Mrs. Reagan testified that your sister said, "Emma, you have given me away, haven't you?" And you replied, "No, Lizzie, I haven't." Then she said, "I won't give in one inch." Was there any such talk any morning?

A. Never.

Be the Jury

Is Emma Borden telling the truth, or lying to save her sister?

Cross-Examination by the Prosecution

The prosecutor targeted an argument five years before between Lizzie and Mrs. Borden, which he believed had spurred Lizzie's hatred and jealousy of her stepmother.

Q. Did your stepmother own a house?

A. Yes. She owned one with her half sister, Mrs. Whitehead. Five years ago my father bought Mrs. Whitehead's half and gave it to my stepmother.

Q. Did that make any trouble between your stepmother and Lizzie and you?

A. Yes, sir.

A newspaper sketch shows the prosecutor cross-examining Emma Borden.

Q. Did you and Lizzie find fault with your father's actions?

A. Yes, sir.

Q. And because of this argument didn't your father give you his grandfather's house, which was worth more than your stepmother's house?

A. Yes he did, but not because of this argument.

Q. Were relations between you and Lizzie and your stepmother as pleasant after that?

A. Between my sister and Mrs. Borden they were entirely the same. But not on my part.

The prosecutor believed that Lizzie's refusal to call Mrs. Borden "Mother" showed her growing hatred toward her stepmother.

Q. From her childhood, your sister called Mrs. Borden "Mother." Didn't she stop calling her "Mother" after this incident?

A. She did stop calling her "Mother," but I can't tell you whether it was at that time or not.

Q. What did she call her after that?

A. Mrs. Borden.

The prosecutor brought in Emma's inquest testimony because it contradicted what she was saying now.

Q. Do you remember at the inquest when I asked, "Were relations entirely friendly between your stepmother and your sister Lizzie?" And you answered, "No."

A. I don't remember that answer. If you said I did, I did, but I don't remember saying it.

Q. Do you remember that I asked you if relations between you and your stepmother were cordial?

A. I think you did.

Q. Miss Borden, do you know of anybody who had ill will toward your stepmother? Or any enemy she had?

A. No, sir.

The next topic was the note supposedly received by Mrs. Borden.

Q. You placed an advertisement in the *News* for several days for the messenger as well as the writer of the note sent to Mrs. Borden to come forward. Did you ever get any response to the notice?

A. No.

The prosecutor's final questions about Lizzie's raincoat hinted that it might have been used as an outer garment to protect her dress from blood.

Q. Where did Miss Lizzie keep her raincoat?

A. In the clothes press at the top of the stairs.

Redirect by the Defense

The defense needed to dispel the idea that Lizzie's raincoat was hidden somewhere because it was stained with blood.

Q. Where was Lizzie's raincoat when the house was searched?

A. Hanging on the clothes press upstairs.

Q. Where is it now?

A. Same place.

Q. Been there ever since?

A. Every day since.

Be the Jury

Whom shall I believe: Emma Borden or Alice Russell?

Whom shall I believe: Emma Borden or Hannah Reagan?

Why would Russell or Reagan lie?

Witness: **Mary A. Raymond**
Direct Examination by the Defense

Mrs. Raymond, a dressmaker, had worked for the Bordens for eight years.

Q. Did you make the light-blue housedress for Miss Lizzie?

A. Yes, I made it with the help of Mrs. Borden and Emma. It took us a few days to make that dress and Lizzie's other pink housedress.

Q. What material was the light-blue dress?

A. Cotton.

Q. Did you know it got paint stained?

A. Yes, I saw the paint on it shortly after it was made.

Cross-Examination by the Prosecution

Q. Dr. Bowen described this light-blue dress as drab. Do you agree?

A. Yes, when it faded it might look drab.

With this last witness, the defense rested its case.

The Chief Justice looked at Lizzie and said, "Lizzie Andrew Borden, although you have been fully heard by counsel, it is your privilege to add any words which you desire to say in person to the jury. You now have the opportunity."

Lizzie rose and looked at the jurors. "I am innocent."

The Defense's Closing Statement

Monday, June 19, 1893

Now that both sides had presented their witnesses, the lawyers made closing statements. They summarized their viewpoints, contradicted and discredited the evidence from the other side, and appealed to the jury's emotions. The defense went first.

 Fifty-nine-year-old George D. Robinson was familiar to almost everyone in the courtroom. He had been the governor of Massachusetts from 1884 to 1886 and was elected to Congress four times. Robinson faced the jury, put both hands on the bar rail-

ing separating him from them and began to speak.

Listen carefully to Robinson's closing. Remember to separate the facts from his emotional presentation, for you must decide the case based on facts, not emotions.

By now you must realize that it is impossible for this young woman to have committed this terrible crime. It is not your business to figure out who did it. You are here to decide: Is she guilty? And though the real criminal may never be found, better a million times that than finding this woman guilty on insufficient evidence. Remember that the law says if a defendant chooses not to testify, you cannot draw an inference of guilt from that choice. You must also leave out of your mind every rumor and report that you heard before the trial began. You must leave out of your mind every single thing that the prosecutor said he would prove unless he has actually proved it. For example, he said he would prove that the defendant prepared a dangerous weapon—poison—the day before the murders. You have not heard any such evidence. It is not proved because the court did not allow it to be proved.

There is absolutely no direct evidence against Miss Borden. There is no weapon. There was not a spot of blood on her or her clothes. Yes, there was one drop of blood on the white skirt, as big as the head of a small pin. Miss Borden had her monthly illness at that time. Professor Wood said he did not know whether the blood on the slip was or was not menstrual blood.

There was no blood on her hair. How could she have murdered them without getting blood on her hair? Dr. Draper testified that it is almost impossible to get blood out of the hair. And if she had tried, her hair would have been wet. And the ladies fanning her face would surely have seen that.

It is said that on a certain step of the staircase, if you look into the guest room, you can see any object on the floor. They say that when Miss Lizzie went downstairs, she must have seen Mrs. Borden lying behind the bed. Now, what if we marched you up and down the stairs and didn't tell you what we wanted you to look at? Do you think you would squint under that bed as you walked down? Of course not.

We agree that Miss Lizzie went up and down the stairs about 9 A.M., when Mrs. Borden was making the bed. But there is not the slightest bit of evidence that the guest-room door was open then. We know the door was open later, but there is no evidence that it was open then.

They say Miss Lizzie lied about Mrs. Borden's getting a note. But you heard Mrs. Churchill say that Bridget told her that Mrs. Borden had a note from someone who was sick. Both Bridget and Lizzie had learned from Mrs. Borden that she had received a note.

The prosecutor and a few other people in the courtroom looked up in surprise at Robinson's last comments, for Bridget had never said that Mrs. Borden had told her about the note. Bridget had said that she learned about the note from Lizzie.

So where is the note? Why hasn't its author come forward? Believe it or not, there are people living in this county who do not know this trial is going on. Often after a trial is over, someone steps forward and says, "Well, if I had really known that that question was in dispute, I could have told you all about it." So why didn't this person come forward sooner? Well, sometimes people, especially women, dread coming into a courtroom. And maybe the note was part of the assassin's scheme. We don't know. All we know is that a note arrived.

Mr. Lubinsky saw Miss Lizzie at the barn.

Miss Lizzie said she was in the barn for twenty or thirty minutes. She told Bridget she was in the backyard at the time of the murder. She told Dr. Bowen she was in the barn looking for some iron for sinkers. She told Miss Russell she went to the barn for a piece of tin or iron to fix her screen. Can't all these things be true?

Remember—she couldn't get to the barn without going through the yard. Is it unreasonable that she stopped there by the pear trees for five or ten minutes? Haven't you ever lingered in your yard on the way to doing a chore?

If she was the archcriminal they claim, her story would be so perfect that she could tell it line for line the same every time. We all know that witnesses who tell the truth often slightly vary their stories. The ones who recite their testimony like parrots are the suspicious ones.

Miss Lizzie said she thought she heard Mrs. Borden come in. The idea that Mrs. Borden had come in was the most natural thought in the world. She probably heard some noise in the house, maybe the shutting of a door—and thought that Mrs. Borden had come in.

They say she showed no feeling when her stepmother was lying dead on the guest-room floor, that she laughed on the stairs. Why shouldn't she laugh? She didn't know Mrs. Borden was dead. She hadn't murdered her. If she had murdered her father, do you think she would have called so quickly for Bridget? They say she didn't show any signs of fear. But she said to Bridget, "You must go and get somebody, for I can't stay in this house alone." Isn't that a cry of distress?

They say Lizzie murdered Mr. Borden for his money, or possibly to hide her crime. Have they proved that? They have proved that five or six years ago Lizzie stopped calling Mrs. Borden "Mother." Is there anything criminal about that? Does the statement "She is not my mother; she is my stepmother" smack of murder?

But what about Lizzie's statement to Mrs. Gifford: "Don't say 'Mother' to me. She is a mean good-for-nothing thing." I agree that that is not a good way to talk. I agree that Lizzie Borden is not a saint. I also know you are not saints, and doubt that you never speak hurriedly or impatiently.

Bridget Sullivan lived with that family almost three years and was nearer to them than anybody else. She never heard any arguing.

On Thursday morning when they say Miss Lizzie was planning the murders, Bridget heard her talking calmly with her stepmother. And Mrs. Raymond testified that all four of them sat together, at a regular dressmaking party, just a few months ago. Was that a murderous group?

They have said that Emma Borden's sisterly affection carried her away from the truth. But what was untrue about her testimony? She admitted that they had trouble six years ago. She said as far as Lizzie was concerned it was all settled.

In his opening the district attorney said that there was an impassable wall between the occupants of the house. But we learned that the doors to everyone's rooms were locked because of a burglary. The impassable wall was not against the two girls. It was simply protection against strangers.

The government says she burned a dress and lied about the dress she wore that morning. But people who saw Lizzie that day disagree about what she wore. Some say she wore a dark blue dress. Mrs. Churchill speaks of it as lighter blue.

The witnesses may disagree about what Lizzie wore, but every single person testified that there was not a spot of blood on her dress, or hands, or face, or hair. So the idea that this dress was burned to hide something is ridiculous. So where was the dress that the police didn't find it? In the closet. Miss Emma saw it there on Saturday night. She told her sister to get rid of it. Was there grease or paint on it? Yes, Lizzie got paint on it in May.

On Sunday, she followed Emma's suggestion. She burned the dress in the kitchen. She did not hide what she was doing. The windows were all open. The police were in the yard. In fact, when Miss Russell said, "I think you have done the worst thing you could in burning that dress," Lizzie said, "Why did you let me do it, then?"

I ask the prosecutors this: If Lizzie Borden killed her stepmother at 9:45 A.M. and then came down to greet her father, why wasn't she covered with blood? Of course the government will say she changed her dress, and then when she killed her father, she either put that dress back on or she put on another. If she put it on again over her clothes and her body, wouldn't her underclothing get soiled? If she put on another dress, then there were two dresses to burn and get rid of, instead of one. The whole matter is physically impossible.

The prosecutor says she murdered these two people because Mrs. Reagan said the sisters quarreled. Supposedly Lizzie said, "Emma, you have given me away." If there is anybody given away in this case, it is Mrs. Reagan.

Lizzie did not try to get Bridget out of the house. She told her about the sale at Sargeant's because it was a good sale. If she wanted her out of the way, she would have sent her on an errand. But instead, everything in the house went on as usual.

Now, back to the weapons. Dr. Draper says the cutting edge of the murder instrument was three and a half inches, but he also says it could have been done by an instrument three inches wide or two and

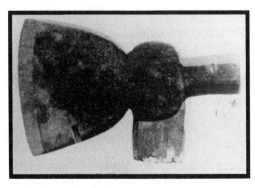

three quarter inches. You see why we do not usually hang people upon the testimony of experts. It isn't safe.

So now we have this broken hatchet. One policeman tells us it had been dropped in ashes and tossed in the box and had fine dust on it. They also say it had coarse dust on it. I am sure it did. I am also sure that you have in your barns and shops and cellars some old things that you haven't thrown away, and that they have dirt and dust and ashes on them.

The prosecutor says that this hatchet was washed thoroughly to get all the blood off. Then the handle was deliberately broken off. Professor Wood could not find the slightest trace of blood. The government says the broken hatchet may have been the weapon. Can you convict this defendant on a theory that it may have been?

They say Lizzie was shut up in that house with the two victims and that everybody else was absolutely shut out. But Bridget told us that the side screen door was unfastened from about 9 A.M. to 10:45 while she was outside.

So what was Lizzie doing during this time? Doing what any decent woman does. Doing what your wives are doing now—ironing handkerchiefs, going up and down the stairs, going down into the cellar, doing the ordinary work around the house.

Now suppose the assassin came in. Lizzie was upstairs or downstairs in the cellar. Where did he go? Upstairs to the spare room, or into the hall closet or the sitting-room closet, or into the pantry. It was easy enough for him to go up to that bedroom and secret himself there until he was ready to murder Mr. Borden. Yes, he came there to murder Mr. Borden. But he found Mrs. Borden, so he killed her.

The prosecution says nobody saw the assassin go in. But nobody saw Mr. Borden leave the house either. And there was somebody about the house. Dr. Handy, Mr. Chase, and Mrs. Hart saw a stranger on the sidewalk just before the murder. This murder was not done by one man alone; there was somebody else in it. The idea of sole opportunity does not hold.

Thomas Barlow and Everett Brown have testified that they were out in that barn before Officer Medley. Medley is wrong when he says there were no tracks in the barn.

Look at Miss Lizzie. To find her guilty you must believe she is a fiend. Does she look it? As she has sat here these long weary days have you seen anything that shows the lack of human feelings? Please give us your verdict of "not guilty" so that the defendant may go home and be Lizzie Andrew Borden of Fall River in that bloodstained and wrecked home where she has passed her life for so many years.

The Prosecution's Closing Statement

Monday, June 19, 1893

Forty-six-year-old Hosea M. Knowlton had been the district attorney of the county for fourteen years. He had served as a state representative and state senator. He was also a partner in a New Bedford law firm. Knowlton faced the jury and began his speech in a quiet voice.

Listen carefully to Knowlton's closing. Remember to separate the facts from his emotional presentation, for you must decide the case based on facts, not emotions.

This was a terrible crime and it is hard to believe that a woman did it. But don't forget, gentlemen; women are humans like us. And the evidence makes it impossible for us not to believe that this woman did this terrible crime.

My learned adversary says we cannot believe circumstantial evidence. But did you ever hear of a murderer getting witnesses to see or hear his work? Murder is committed in secret. There have been very few cases where there was direct testimony. If we dismiss this case because it relies on circumstantial evidence, then no murder case can be tried, and murder goes unpunished.

The issue is not circumstantial evidence. It is whether or not there is enough circumstantial evidence. What is called circumstantial evidence is nothing in the world but a presumption of circumstances. There is no chain about it. The word "chain" is incorrectly used as applied to this. Let's take an example of circumstantial evidence.

Let us take the burning of that light-blue dress. No one witnessed it. Nobody told us they saw Lizzie Andrew Borden burn that dress. And yet the defense never said to you, "That evidence is circumstantial and you cannot believe it because there were no witnesses." We heard what the prisoner said before the act was supposed to have taken place. We heard what she said after the fact. We put these circumstances together and say that the dress was burned. Her lawyers do not deny it even though there were no witnesses.

Dear jurors, it is not a question of circumstantial evidence; it is a question as to whether there is enough circumstantial evidence.

There was no peace or harmony in this family. The prisoner said to Mrs. Gifford, "Don't say 'Mother' to me. She is a mean good-for-nothing old thing." That statement tells it all. And so does the prisoner's correcting Mr. Fleet that Mrs. Borden was not her mother, at the very moment when the poor woman who had reared her lay dead within ten feet of her voice.

The family did not eat together. Bridget said so. Lizzie's uncle never saw her when he visited. I admire Miss Emma's loyalty. Her only sister is in danger. She must come to her rescue, so she tells us that family relations were peaceful. But we sadly know they were not. She tells us that she told her sister to destroy the dress. Her evidence is different from Miss Russell's. Emma Borden tells us that Mrs. Reagan did not hear the two sisters quarrel in the jail. You have got to decide whether to believe Miss Emma or Miss Russell, Miss Emma or Mrs. Reagan.

Every door in this house was locked, so how could anyone have gotten in when Mr. Borden left?

My learned friend has spent much time showing that the prisoner could not see her murdered mother as she went up and down the stairs. But where was she that she couldn't hear the force of Mrs. Borden's two hundred pounds when she fell flat on the floor? Do you believe that those blows could have been struck without Mrs. Borden's groaning or screaming, and that Lizzie knew nothing about it?

Lizzie lied when she said that Mrs. Borden received a note and left. My learned friend says someone else wrote that note. Gentlemen of the jury, do you believe that any friend of Mrs. Borden's would not have rushed to tell us that she wrote the note?

My learned friend suggests that the note was part of the assassin's plan. But why write a note to get Mrs. Borden away from the house when he went there to kill her? Why write a note to get rid of her and leave Lizzie and Bridget there to watch the murders?

My learned adversary has said that there is no motive for this crime. But hate had gone on under that roof for many, many years. How do we explain the horrible fact that a daughter killed her father? I say Andrew Borden's daughter never came down those stairs. It was not Lizzie Borden but a murderer, transformed into a criminal. Lizzie killed her father because he would have known that she had killed Mrs. Borden. And he would not have hidden this tragedy.

Let us examine some important facts in this case. First, why did the prisoner iron on this extremely hot day? Why didn't she wait until it cooled down? She was ironing in the dining room when Bridget went upstairs to rest. She was alone with her father. Supposedly the fire wasn't hot enough and she stopped ironing. Twenty minutes later, she called Bridget and told her that her father was killed.

At 12:30 Officer Harrington saw a fire in the kitchen stove. If there was fire enough to be seen at 12:30, there was fire enough for ironing an hour and a half before. After all, it was just a little job— eight or nine handkerchiefs. They could be ironed in less than ten minutes. Why did she stop ironing them?

After the murders, everyone asked Lizzie the same question: "Where were you when your father was killed?" How did she answer? She said she had been in the barn for thirty minutes getting a piece of iron for sinkers or tin to fix her screen. That story is unbelievable and absurd. You are asked to believe that on a day when the temperature soared to one hundred degrees, she left her ironing and went to that stifling hot barn for thirty minutes just when the assassin killed her father.

And if she did go there to get sinkers or material to fix a screen, show us proof. Show us the broken screen, show us the sinkers. This alibi does not stand. Officer Medley found no footprints anywhere in that dusty barn loft. She wasn't there. She said she was there because it was the only place she could be and not have known or heard what took place.

But what about Mr. Lubinsky's testimony that he saw Miss Lizzie coming out of the barn? Mr. Gardiner told us that at 11 A.M. Mr. Lubinsky's horse was being fed. So by the time Mr. Lubinsky passed the Borden house and glanced into the yard, it was probably 11:15. And by that time, Lizzie was in the house. Mr. Lubinsky might have seen Mrs. Churchill, or Bridget, or Alice Russell. But he did not see Lizzie.

I completely dismiss the testimony of the two boys, Everett Brown and Thomas Barlow.

Here is another strange thing I cannot understand. When Lizzie came into the sitting room and saw that foul murder, she could not know if the assassin was still there or had escaped. And yet she never cried out for help. She never left that house. She never even went out on the steps. She stood inside the screen door and calmly asked Bridget to go get her friends. How strange.

Of course the question naturally arises: "How could she have avoided spattering her dress with blood if she did these crimes?" I cannot answer it. You cannot answer it. The assassin's cunning is beyond me. Concealment is part of an assassin's business. Maybe the old man's coat which was folded up on his cushion was put over the dress. There are many ways to protect a dress.

We do not know how she kept the dress from being spattered, but we do know that she did not wear the dark-blue silk dress that morning. Do your wives dress in silk to iron on the hottest day of the year? No, no. Mrs. Churchill described Lizzie's morning dress as a light-blue and white cotton with a dark diamond on it. When I showed her the dark-blue silk, she said she did not see Lizzie wear it that morning.

The defense says that the light-blue cotton dress had been stained with paint since May. I believe it. But the paint had not stopped the prisoner from wearing it for four months. It was good enough for a housedress, good enough for an ironing dress, good enough for doing chores.

On Thursday the police searched the house. On Saturday afternoon, when they searched the closets, why didn't they see this paint-stained dress? Emma tells us it was in that closet. But the police didn't find it. They didn't find it because it was hidden somewhere.

We produced a hatchet that was deliberately broken off so that no part of the wood of the handle was left. Professor Wood tells us that the hatchet was covered with ashes. He says it could have been cleaned after having been used. This hatchet miraculously fits to the dot the cuts on the dead man's skull. Now we do not say that that was the murder hatchet, but it may well have been.

Finally let us get back to this mysterious, unknown assassin who the defense has suggested did the murders. He came into the house when there was no way to get in. He hid in closets where the police found no blood. He went from room to room though no traces of blood were found in the hallways or on the stairs. He knew that Bridget would go upstairs to sleep when she didn't know it beforehand. He knew that Lizzie would go to the barn when she couldn't have known it. He knew that Mrs. Borden would be upstairs. Do you think this assassin would have taken away a bloody weapon? Never. He never would have gone into the streets with it. He would have left it beside his victim's body. But no hatchet was found in the house. That piece of evidence points directly to a person living in that house as author of this awful crime.

After Mr. Borden's body was discovered and Bridget offered to go to Mrs. Borden's sister to see if Mrs. Borden was there, Lizzie told her that she was almost positive that she had heard Mrs. Borden come in. If she had heard her come in, why didn't she call out to her on the second floor about her husband's murder instead of calling out to the domestic on the third floor? She didn't account for Mrs. Borden until things began to crowd around her.

This case has all the elements of crime—hatred, spite, and an absurd and impossible alibi. We have contradictory stories that cannot be verified. We have fraud by substituting an afternoon silk dress for one supposedly worn that morning. And we have Lizzie's housedress, important evidence destroyed so that the microscope cannot find any blood on it.

So what is the defense? Nothing, I say again, nothing. They have thrown some dust on Mrs. Reagan's story. They have told us some absurd stories about men standing quietly on the street the same day of the tragedy. But other than that—nothing, nothing.

"WHAT IS THE DEFENSE? NOTHING, NOTHING, NOTHING."

Brilliant and Convincing Argument of District Attorney Knowlton Brought To a Close at Noon.

Headlines from *The Sun*

The Judge's Charge
Tuesday, June 20, 1893

After the lawyers finished their closing statements, Justice Dewey talked to the jury. He *charged* (instructed) the jurors with the law. He explained how the law applied to this case, and how they must follow it in reaching their verdict. A judge's charge is supposed to be impartial—favoring neither one side nor the other.

The government claims that the Borden murders were premeditated, and that it was murder in the first degree. The government must show the defendant had motives for these homicides. We have learned that Mr. Borden's $300,000 estate will be inherited by the defendant and her sister. The government claims that the defendant had ill will toward her stepmother, nearly, if not quite, amounting to hatred. Her remarks to Mrs. Gifford are largely the basis for that claim.

Use caution when evaluating testimony about conversations. For example, do the defendant's remarks to Mrs. Gifford mean what the government said they mean? Don't young women often use intense expression, sometimes admiration, sometimes dislike? Don't young women often use words which, if strictly taken, would go far beyond their real meanings?

To get a true picture of the defendant's feelings toward her mother, you must consider Mrs. Gifford's testimony along with testimony by Bridget Sullivan, Emma Borden, and Mrs. Raymond. You must think about how the family lived. Whether they sewed together and went to church together. In a word, the tone of their life. Weigh all testimony carefully before deciding whether it was clearly proved that the defendant's state of mind toward her stepmother provides a real motive to kill her.

This case is based upon circumstantial evidence. No witnesses testified to seeing the defendant commit the crime. This is a legal and not unusual way of proving a criminal case, and juries may find a person guilty of murder upon circumstantial evidence alone. You have heard many facts by many witnesses. You must decide what facts have been proved. Then you must decide what conclusions can be drawn from the facts. Every fact that is important and essential for deciding the defendant's guilt must be proved beyond a reasonable doubt.

For example, the government claims that the defendant deliberately lied about her stepmother's receiving a note. The prosecutors point out that the person who wrote the note has not been found, and the person who delivered it has not been found. The note also has not been found. Think about this. If the defendant were guilty, why would she make up a story that would be difficult to explain later on? If there was another assassin, couldn't the note be part of his plan to get Mrs. Borden out of the house? And after he killed her, might he not have removed the note so it couldn't be traced to him?

Look at the matter from one side. Then look at it from the other. Never assume beforehand that the defendant is guilty. Does the evidence satisfy you beyond any reasonable doubt that the defendant's statements about that note are necessarily false?

For a conviction based on circumstantial evidence, the government does not have to show that by no possibility was it in the power of any other person than the defendant to commit the crimes.

But the evidence must produce a conviction amounting to a reasonable and moral certainty that the defendant and no one else did commit them. Is there anything in the manner of the killing which tells us about the sex and strength of the murderer? Is it reasonable and believable that the defendant could have killed Mrs. Borden, plotted killing her father later, and spent the time in between murders with no change in manner to excite attention?

The prosecutor challenges the defendant's statement that she was in the barn loft. The prosecutor claims that story cannot be believed because of the extreme heat in the loft and because one officer found no tracks in the dust. Weigh this evidence carefully.

Different people have told us what the defendant said about her whereabouts when her father was being murdered. She said different things to each of these people. I remind you that frequently people unintentionally change a few words and give a very different impression from what they actually said. If the defendant is to be held responsible largely upon her statements, then those statements must be thoroughly proved.

You have heard that the defendant predicted disaster in her household. The prosecutor believes that Miss Borden's statements to Miss Russell show that she was harboring evil thoughts about her parents. Think about this: Is it reasonable and probable that a person planning such a great crime would on the day before, predict it to a friend?

As for the matter of the dress she wore that day. Can you figure out from what various people have said, what her dress looked like? Do people agree about what she wore?

A last point. The defendant chose not to testify. The law says that a person has the right not to furnish evidence against himself. No conclusions can be drawn from the fact that someone decides not to testify. So remember, you cannot have any unfavorable thoughts about the defendant because she didn't testify.

If, after weighing the evidence carefully, you are convinced beyond a reasonable doubt of the defendant's guilt, you must return a verdict of "guilty." If the evidence does not convince you beyond a reasonable doubt, even a strong probability of guilt, you must return a verdict of "not guilty."

The case is now committed into your hands. You will now enter the jury room and deliberate.

Be the Jury

The jury began deliberating at 3:02 P.M. on June 20, 1893. They probably discussed the following questions:

Has the prosecutor proved Lizzie guilty beyond a reasonable doubt?

Go over what each prosecution witness said. Did you believe the witness? Did the cross-examination prove that the testimony was false or unreliable?

Go over what each defense witness said. Did you believe the witness? Did the cross-examination prove that the testimony was false or unreliable?

When jurors review evidence to determine

facts, they may call in the court stenographer to read testimony, and the lawyers' and judges' statements, back to them. At any point in your deliberations, you may turn back to clarify the testimony. Use the Stenographer's Notes to locate specific points.

When you have reached your verdict, turn the page to see what Lizzie Borden's jury decided.

The Verdict

At 4:32 P.M., after one and a half hours of de-liberation, the jury returned to the courtroom.

A magazine illustration showing Lizzie and her defense lawyer waiting for the verdict.

The clerk asked Lizzie to stand. When she rose, he turned to the jury and asked, "Gentlemen of the jury, have you agreed upon your verdict?"

"Yes, we have," said the foreman.

The foreman gave the paper with the verdict on it to the clerk, who gave it to the Chief Justice. He looked at it and then the clerk returned it to the foreman. The clerk said, "Mr. Foreman, look upon the prisoner: Prisoner, look upon the foreman. What say you, Mr. Foreman . . . "

"Not guilty," the foreman interrupted before the clerk was finished with his question.

Lizzie sat back quickly in her chair and covered her face with her hands. People in the courtroom yelled and waved hats and handkerchiefs. Lizzie cried uncontrollably. Her sister and friends hugged her. Andrew Jennings shook the hands of the other defense lawyers. "Thank God, oh, thank God," Jennings said.

An hour later, when Lizzie stepped into her carriage, the crowd cheered her. Men and women shook her hand. Her carriage pulled away to the train station and Lizzie went home to Fall River.

> ## LIZZIE BORDEN FREE.
>
> ---
>
> ### A Verdict of Acquittal Received Tumultuously in Court.
>
> ---
>
> #### VINDICATED, SHE BREAKS DOWN.
>
> ---
>
> An Extraordinary Scene in the New, Bedford Court Room

Headlines from *The Sun*

Lizzie and Emma moved to a large house at 306 French Street, in a better part of Fall River. Lizzie called the new home Maplecroft and had the name carved on the stone steps. Lizzie changed her name to Lisbeth A. Borden.

Lizzie continued attending church but withdrew from other social activities. Despite community support during the trial, for the next thirty-four years Lizzie was ostracized in the town. She was rarely seen in public, except in her carriage. She visited Boston and Washington, D.C., frequently because no one recognized her there.

She became news again in 1897, when a woman took a painting into a store in Providence, Rhode Island, for repair. When the manager asked where she had gotten the painting, the woman told her that Lizzie Borden of Fall River had given it to her as a gift. The painting had been missing from the store and assumed stolen. A warrant was issued for Lizzie. Lizzie's lawyers settled the matter out of court; the warrant was never served.

In 1904, Lizzie and her sister had an argument over Lizzie's invitation to actress Nancy O'Neil and her theatrical troupe to their home. Emma moved out of the house and away from Fall River.

Lizzie died in 1927 at the age of sixty-seven. She left $30,000 to the Animal Rescue League of Fall River and $80,000 in smaller sums to friends, distant relatives, and servants.

Guilty or Innocent?

The Lizzie Borden case has been written about by many people—lawyers, police reporters, mystery buffs.

Many people believe Lizzie was acquitted because in 1893 the jury of twelve men just couldn't accept the idea that a wealthy churchgoing woman could have committed these brutal murders. At the turn of the century, women were thought of as the "weaker sex." Women were seen as loving, kind, gentle, and incapable of violence. In addition, the idea that a daughter would kill her father was too shocking an idea for most people to believe.

Many people said that Judge Dewey's charge was improper and was a plea for Lizzie's innocence instead of an instruction to help the jury understand the law. These critics say that Judge Dewey dismissed the importance of Lizzie's remarks to Mrs. Gifford. As for the question of the missing note, they point out that the judge seemed to imply that Lizzie wouldn't have made up a story that couldn't be proved, and that perhaps the note was part of an assassin's scheme. As for Lizzie's conversation with Alice Russell, Judge Dewey seemed to belittle its importance in showing Lizzie's state of mind.

Most people agree the evidence was strong that the dress Lizzie wore that morning was missing and was not the dress she gave to the police; however, the prosecutor did not conclusively prove that the light-blue housedress that Lizzie had burned was the dress she had worn that morning. The prosecutor also didn't emphasize that the blue silk dress that Lizzie had said she had worn that morning was a heavy winter silk, totally inappropriate for summer wear, especially in a heat wave.

Many people believe that the piece of evidence that acquitted Lizzie was the fact that five people who saw her within fifteen minutes after the second murder saw not a drop of blood on her clothes, her hair, her face, or her body. One expert witness said it was practically impossible for someone to have dealt the twenty-nine blows to both victims without getting some blood on her clothes or person.

What Do You Think?

If Lizzie didn't do it, who did, and how was it done?

If Lizzie did do it, how did she do it?

What If ?

What if Lizzie Had Been Tried Today?

If Lizzie had been tried today, some trial evidence would have been different. Most likely today's police would do a thorough search of Lizzie's person, clothes, shoes, and stockings the day of the murder, so the questions of which dress she wore and whether she had any traces of blood on her person or clothing would have been resolved. The police would have dusted for fingerprints on the handleless hatchet and on doorknobs and other objects the murderer might have touched.

If Lizzie had been tried today, there would have been women on the jury.

If Lizzie had been tried today, the fact that she was a woman would not have been reason to believe her innocent.

Author's Note

The testimony in this book was edited from the transcript of Lizzie Borden's trial and from newspaper articles that reprinted the testimony at the time.

The descriptions of people and interactions in the courtroom were taken from newspaper articles.

For purposes of economy, as in the testimony of Bridget Sullivan, many questions and answers were combined. Also for purposes of economy, not all trial evidence was included in this book. But the most important facts and contradictions have been included to give a balanced picture so that you could be a fair juror.

Acknowledgments

I thank Alan H. Levine, who took time from his busy teaching schedule—and from his commitment to providing legal protection for all Americans—to read the manuscript. Danielle Weekes, Jessica Castro, Robyn German, Jeryna Hailstock, and Melonie Everett of Linda Margolin's fifth-grade class at P.S. 84 in New York, and Alexandra Weininger of Josephine Kono's sixth-grade class at Montgomery C. Smith Middle School in Hudson, New York, brought their special expertise to reading this book. Florence C. Brigham of the Fall River Historical Society helped me to secure many of the photographs. The New York Public Library provided space in the Wertheim Study to facilitate my research, and the library staff, as always, proved tireless in answering all requests. Christine Kettner generously let me intrude on her graphic design. My gratitude to my editor, Katherine Brown Tegen, who helped give birth to this series, is boundless.

Bibliography

Books

The starred books are particularly appropriate for young readers.

*David, Andrew. *Famous Supreme Court Cases*. Minneapolis, Minn.: Lerner Publications, 1980.

*——— *Famous Criminal Trials*. Minneapolis, Minn.: Lerner Publications, 1979.

*Gustafson, Anita. *Guilty or Innocent*. New York: Holt, Rinehart & Winston, 1985.

Lewis, Anthony. *Gideon's Trumpet*. New York: Vintage Books, 1964.

Lincoln, Victoria. *A Private Disgrace: Lizzie Borden by Daylight*. New York: International Polygonics, 1986.

Pearson, Edmund, ed. *Trial of Lizzie Borden*. New York: Doubleday, Doran & Company, 1937.

Radin, Edward D. *Lizzie Borden: The Untold Story*. New York: Simon & Schuster, 1961.

Sullivan, Robert. *Good-bye Lizzie Borden*. Brattleboro, Vermont: The Stephen Greene Press, 1974.

Wigmore, John L. *The American Law Review*, Volume 27, November–December 1893.

*Zerman, Melvyn B. *Beyond a Reasonable Doubt: Inside the American Jury System.* New York: Thomas Y. Crowell Company, 1981.

Newspapers

Boston Evening Standard
Boston Morning Journal
New York Daily Tribune

Stenographer's Notes

These notes cover only testimony accepted at the trial because that is all you, as jury members, are allowed to see.

Page numbers in *italics* refer to illustrations.

Doreen Rappaport

is the author of many books for children, including LIVING DANGEROUSLY: *American Women Who Risked Their Lives for Adventure*; ESCAPE FROM SLAVERY: *Five Journeys to Freedom*; THE BOSTON COFFEE PARTY; TROUBLE AT THE MINES, an Honor Book for the 1988 Jane Addams Children's Book Award; and AMERICAN WOMEN: *Their Lives in Their Words*, a 1990 Notable Children's Trade Book in the Field of Social Studies and a 1992 ALA Best Book for Young Adults. THE SACCO-VANZETTI TRIAL is another title in Ms. Rappaport's BE THE JUDGE • BE THE JURY™ series.

Ms. Rappaport is also the creator of award-winning educational programs focusing on American history, literature, and music. She lives in New York City.